my **revisi⏻n** notes

AS AQA History
USA
1890–1945

Neil Ashworth

John Spiller

Series editors:

Robin Bunce and
Laura Gallagher

HODDER
EDUCATION
AN HACHETTE UK COMPANY

The Publishers would like to thank the following for permission to reproduce copyright material:

Acknowledgements

AQA material is reproduced by permission of AQA.

Every effort has been made to trace all copyright holders, but if any have been inadvertently overlooked the Publishers will be pleased to make the necessary arrangements at the first opportunity.

Although every effort has been made to ensure that website addresses are correct at time of going to press, Hodder Education cannot be held responsible for the content of any website mentioned in this book. It is sometimes possible to find a relocated web page by typing in the address of the home page for a website in the URL window of your browser.

Hachette UK's policy is to use papers that are natural, renewable and recyclable products and made from wood grown in sustainable forests. The logging and manufacturing processes are expected to conform to the environmental regulations of the country of origin.

Orders: please contact Bookpoint Ltd, 130 Milton Park, Abingdon, Oxon OX14 4SB.
Telephone: +44 (0)1235 827720. Fax: +44 (0)1235 400454. Lines are open 9.00a.m.–5.00p.m., Monday to Saturday, with a 24-hour message answering service. Visit our website at www.hoddereducation.co.uk

© Neil Ashworth, John Spiller 2014
First published in 2014 by
Hodder Education,
An Hachette UK Company
338 Euston Road
London NW1 3BH

Impression number   10 9 8 7 6 5 4 3 2 1
Year   2018 2017 2016 2015 2014

Cover photo © 2000 Topham Picturepoint/TopFoto
Artwork by Datapage (India) Pvt. Ltd.
Typeset in 11/13 Stempel Schneidler Std-Light by Datapage (India) Pvt. Ltd.
Printed in India

A catalogue record for this title is available from the British Library

ISBN 978 14441 99703

Contents

Introduction

About Unit 1

Unit 1 is worth 50 per cent of your AS level. It requires an understanding of change and continuity over time and an awareness of cause and consequence within a broad historical context. There are no sources in the Unit 1 examination and therefore all marks available are awarded for your own knowledge and understanding.

In the examination, you are required to answer two questions out of three and each question has two parts. The first part, worth 12 marks, asks you to explain why an event, issue or development occurred. Twelve-mark questions begin 'Explain why' or 'Why did'. The second part, worth 24 marks, requires a balanced evaluation and begins 'How far', 'How important' or 'How successful'. The examination lasts for 1 hour and 15 minutes, unless you have been awarded extra time. You are advised to spend 12 minutes on the first part of each question and 25 minutes on the second part.

The examination will test your own knowledge and understanding of the period and requires you to:

■ refer to relevant historical information

■ demonstrate an understanding of change and continuity

■ show an awareness that events and developments are open to differing interpretations

■ use good English, organise information clearly and use specialist vocabulary where appropriate.

USA, 1890–1945

The specification lists the content of Unit 1: USA, 1890–1945 under the following broad headings:

1. The USA, 1890–c1920
2. The USA, c1920–1929
3. The Great Depression and the New Deal, 1929–1941
4. The Impact of the Second World War on the USA, 1941–1945

How to use this book

This book has been designed to help you to develop the knowledge and skills necessary to succeed in the examination of this unit. The book is divided into four sections – one for each section of the unit. Each section is made up of a series of topics organised into double-page spreads. On the left-hand page, you will find a summary of the key content you need to learn. Words in bold in the key content are defined in the glossary (see pages 70–71). On the right-hand page, you will find exam-focused activities. Together, these two strands of the book will provide you with the knowledge and skills essential for examination success.

▼ Key historical content   ▼ Exam-focused activities

There are two types of examination activities focusing on the two types of examination questions.

- ■ 'Explain why' 12-mark answers have this symbol:
- ■ 'How far', 'How important' and 'How successful' 24-mark answers have this symbol:

Some activities have answers or suggested answers on pages 73–78 and have this symbol:

Each section ends with an exam-style question and model A grade answer with examiner's commentary. This will give you guidance on what is expected to achieve the top grade.

You can also keep track of your revision by ticking off each topic heading in the book, or by ticking the checklist on the contents page. Tick each box when you have:

- ■ revised and understood a topic
- ■ completed the activities.

Mark scheme

For some of the activities in the book it will be useful to refer to the mark scheme for the unit. Below is an abbreviated form of the mark scheme for Unit 1.

Assessing 'Explain why' questions			
Level and marks	Approach	Detail	Understanding
Level 1 1–2	Descriptive/generalised		
Level 2 3–6	Descriptive or limited (1–2 factors)	Little supporting evidence	
Level 3 7–9	Range of factors (3 adequate)	Some supporting evidence	
Level 4 10–12	Range of factors (3 adequate)	Precise supporting evidence	Makes links between factors, prioritises them with justification, or identifies types of factor

Assessing 'How far', 'How important' and 'How successful' questions				
Level and marks	Knowledge	Understanding	Balance of interpretations	Judgement
Level 1 1–6	Limited detail or a little description	Generalised comment or assertion		
Level 2 7–11	Some detail or some description	Some (limited) explicit links or comment		
Level 3 12–16	Suitable detail/lacks depth	Explicit links/lacks weight	Maybe some balance	
Level 4 17–21	Good range of detail	Explicit understanding	Balanced argument	
Level 5 22–24	Precise detail	Explicit understanding	Well-balanced argument	Judgement

Section 1:
The USA, 1890–c1920

The US political system in 1890 and the role of the President

Revised

The US Constitution

The US Constitution sets out:

- the structure of government, including the roles of the different branches
- the role of state governments
- the rights of individuals.

It is a sovereign document written in 1787, and pre-dates the election of the first president and Congress. It created a federal system of government and the separation of powers.

Federalism

The USA has a federal system of government, meaning that power is divided between central government and local state governments. Each state can make its own laws and has its own rights, but all have to give up some of their powers to the federal (central) government based in Washington DC. In 1890 the USA had 44 states; today there are 50.

Separation of powers

The federal government has three different branches:

- the Executive – concerned with policy making and headed by the President
- the Legislature – concerned with the framing and passing of laws and called Congress
- the Judiciary – comprises courts and judges and includes the Supreme Court.

The Executive

The President is the most important figure in the executive branch of government. He:

- can **veto** a law passed by Congress (see below)
- makes federal appointments, including cabinet jobs such as Secretary of State, and Supreme Court judges
- is Commander-in-Chief of the armed forces
- takes key foreign policy decisions, such as making treaties, with the backing of the Senate
- initiates legislative programmes aimed at dealing with domestic affairs.

The USA does, however, have a system of **checks and balances** which can sometimes make it difficult for a president to get his own way.

Presidents, 1890–1945

Presidents are chosen every four years by an electoral college at **fixed term elections**. Unlike today, between 1890 and 1945 there was no constitutional limit on the number of terms a president could serve. Most presidents, however, never sought more than two terms in office, in line with the tradition established by George Washington. Three presidents died in office during the period 1890–1945 and were replaced by their vice-presidents.

Presidents between 1890 and 1945 had to contend with major wars, huge economic problems, social division and inequality.

The Legislature

Congress is the **bicameral** legislature of the USA, made up of the Senate and the House of Representatives. Senators are elected for six-year terms, and congressmen only for two years at a time. The number of terms they can serve is not limited. Both houses are responsible for passing new laws and can override a presidential veto with two-thirds majorities. Congress also has the power to **impeach** a president and put him on trial should the need arise.

The Judiciary

The Supreme Court is the highest court in the judicial system of the USA. It is made up of senior judges who have the power to strike down laws passed by Congress if they feel they go against the rules contained within the Constitution.

Political parties

There are two main political parties in the USA, the Republicans and the Democrats. By the 1920s the Republicans were very firmly identified with the interests of big business and *laissez-faire* policies, while the Democrats supported more government intervention to help the less well-off. The Republicans were generally better supported in the industrial North while Democrats were stronger in the less urbanised South. Occasionally other parties managed to poll high numbers of votes at elections, such as the Progressive Party in 1912, when Theodore Roosevelt stood as its candidate.

Mind map

Use the information on the opposite page to add detail to the mind map below.

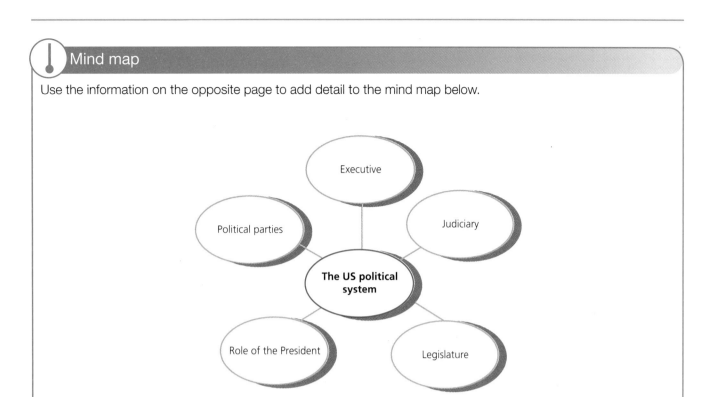

Turning assertion into argument   ⓐ

Below are a sample exam-style 24-mark question and a series of assertions. Read the question and then add a justification to each of the assertions to turn it into a supported view, so creating an argument.

How far were the powers of the presidents in the period 1890–1920 limited?

US presidents in the period 1890–1920 had considerable power over foreign policy ...

_____

_____

US presidents had considerable power over legislation ...

_____

_____

US presidents had considerable powers of patronage ...

_____

_____

Presidential elections

Presidential elections and terms in office

President	Term in office	Elections won
Benjamin Harrison (Rep)	1889–1893	1888
Grover Cleveland (Dem)	1893–1897	1892
William McKinley (Rep)	1897–1901	1896 1900
Theodore Roosevelt (Rep)	1901–1909	1904
William Taft (Rep)	1909–1913	1908
Woodrow Wilson (Dem)	1913–1921	1912 1916
Warren Harding (Rep)	1921–1923	1920
Calvin Coolidge (Rep)	1923–1929	1924
Herbert Hoover (Rep)	1929–1933	1928
Franklin Roosevelt (Dem)	1933–1945	1932 1936 1940 1944
Harry Truman (Dem)	1945–1953	1948

Party policies

Economic

The Republicans tended to support the **gold standard** which big business, rich farmers and urban workers liked, while the Democrats favoured the **free coinage** of silver which helped poor farmers and rural areas. The Republicans took a *laissez-faire* approach on some aspects of the economy such as tax, but also adopted an apparently contradictory protectionist high **tariffs** policy to shield American industry from foreign competition. Democrats tended to favour lower tariffs which generally made goods cheaper for the consumer. Big business gave $3.5 million to the McKinley campaign in 1896 and anarchist Emma Goldman described him as the 'president of the money kings and trust magnates'.

Foreign policy

The Republicans generally followed a more expansionist foreign policy which appealed to many voters because they believed it would bring economic benefits to the country. The Democrats at times pursued an anti-imperialist policy which won them support, such as when Wilson was elected president in 1916 on an anti-war stance, although he still ended up taking the USA into the First World War in 1917.

Electioneering

The importance of having a good campaign manager and fundraiser became increasingly significant in presidential elections. Mark Hanna, who managed McKinley's campaigns in 1896 and 1900, is often credited with the invention of modern electioneering techniques, which included posters which illustrated clear distinctions between what the two main parties stood for. An election poster from 1900 suggested that if people voted for McKinley, American factories would thrive, and people could confidently invest their money in the banks.

Candidate profiles and the electoral college

Being a well-known figure could boost a candidate's chances of victory in an election. William McKinley was a Civil War veteran, and Theodore Roosevelt fought with distinction in Cuba in the Spanish-American War, which had made them national figures before they ran for the presidency. Having the backing of the more populated states in the North East could also help to swing an election; for example in 1896 McKinley would not have become president if he had not won New York State which had the highest number of electoral college votes (36) and Pennsylvania which had the second highest (32).

The mood of the country and particular circumstances

The mood of the country could have a big impact on election results, for example in 1896 many Americans sympathised with the plight of the Cubans and voted for McKinley because he seemed likely to help the Cubans fight off Spanish control. In addition, the Democrats were still blamed for the economic crisis of 1893. In 1920 voters who were disillusioned by US involvement in the First World War and the subsequent peace-making process turned against Wilson's 'idealism' and backed Harding's **'normalcy'** (see page 34).

Prioritisation

Below are a sample exam-style 12-mark question and a list of reasons that could be used in the answer. Demonstrating prioritisation is one way of structuring the answer to an 'Explain why' question. Using your own knowledge and the information on the opposite page, decide the order of priority you would give to these factors. Write numbers on the spectrum below to indicate their relative importance and, beneath each, briefly justify that factor's placement, demonstrating why you feel some factors are more important than others.

Explain why Republican candidates won all the presidential elections between 1896 and 1908.

1. Economic factors
2. Foreign policy
3. Electioneering
4. Candidate profiles
5. The electoral college vote
6. Mood of the country and particular circumstances

Most important   Least important

1	6	2	4	5	3

Turning statements into reasons

Below are a sample exam-style 12-mark question and a series of statements. Read the question and turn each of the statements into a relevant reason that could be used in the answer. The definitions below should help you:

- **Statement**: a fact or an opinion which is not supported by a reason

- **Reason:** a statement which explains or justifies something.

Explain why McKinley won the election of 1896.

STATEMENT	REASON
McKinley's campaign was well funded and well organised.	Mark Hanna - patrons big business $3.5million
The Republicans supported the gold standard and *laissez-faire* economic policies.	Big business, new tensions & wtion workers
The Democrats supported the free coinage of silver and lower tariffs.	benefited only low paid farmers.
McKinley's foreign policy seemed likely to help the Cubans.	Yellow Press, 'sinking of Maine'
McKinley won New York State.	highest no. of electoral colleges
The Democrats were in power when the panic and downturn of 1893 happened.	blamed on Dems.

Mass immigration and its impact on US society and politics

Before the American Civil War (1861–1865), most immigrants had come from Britain and Ireland, Germany and Scandinavia. From about 1880, however, Austro-Hungarians, Italians and Russians accounted for the largest immigrant groups. In the 1890s about 4 million immigrants came to the USA.

The impact of immigration

Economic impact

■ Immigrants provided some of the most famous entrepreneurs and businessmen of the period, such as the Scottish-born Andrew Carnegie, and the Hungarian-born newspaper owner Josef Pulitzer.

■ Immigrants also made up the huge cheap labour force needed to turn the USA into the world's foremost industrial power.

'**New immigrants**' from eastern and southern Europe often had low standards of education and little money. They were easily exploited through the low wages and poor conditions offered by employers, as well as by the '**boss**' and '**padrone**' **systems**. The disparate ethnic groups slowed down the development of strong unions so their welfare and rights were not protected. Immigrant workers tended to drive down wages, and were used to break strikes, such as when Slavic miners were brought into the Pennsylvania anthracite mines and, upon their arrival, had stones thrown at them by the striking Catholic Irish miners. Immigrants were also accused of taking jobs which native-born Americans could have filled, for example Catholic Italians were employed in large numbers on the New York subway system.

Political impact

Anti-immigration **nativist** groups, such as the Immigration Restriction League, the **American Protective Association (APA)** and the Ku Klux Klan (KKK), campaigned against certain immigrant groups on grounds of racial or religious difference. The APA, and KKK, when it revived post-First World War, demanded that Catholics be barred from political office and from working as teachers, and were also very **anti-Semitic**.

Many newly-arrived immigrants in New York had to rely on support from the Tammany Hall. This political organisation would help them to find accommodation and work in return for the immigrants voting Democrat at election time. Tammany came to be seen as a stronghold of the Catholic Irish. The politicians in control of such political machines were called bosses, were often corrupt and could become extremely powerful. Richard Croker was boss of Tammany in the 1890s and used his position to secure the election of his favoured candidate Robert Van Wyck as mayor of New York in 1897. Rumours of Catholic conspiracies, which aimed to bring the USA under the control of the Pope, abounded.

Many Americans came to associate immigrants with political corruption or extremist political views. For example, Emma Goldman was a Lithuanian Jew who was a prominent anarchist during the period.

Social impact

Immigrants were blamed for a whole range of social ills:

■ The overcrowded slums of the Lower East Side of Manhattan were well publicised in Jacob Riis's 1890 book *How the Other Half Lives*.

■ **Temperance groups** blamed immigrant groups such as the Germans for problems linked to alcohol.

■ Immigrants in the poorer districts of cities were often linked to high crime rates.

■ Gangs such as Paul Kelly's Italian 'Five Pointers' inhabited New York.

■ The 1891 Immigration Act was enforced to stop immigrants bringing in contagious diseases, but despite tougher checks at Ellis Island, cholera and TB outbreaks were frequent in the overcrowded cities.

It could be argued that in the longer term immigrants brought with them a diversity of culture and religion which only enriched the country, but at the time the findings of the Dillingham Commission focused on the perceived problems of immigrants not assimilating and not sharing US values, which tended to reflect the beliefs of many native-born Americans.

Economic, political or social factors?

Below is a sample exam-style 12-mark question which asks for a range of reasons. Understanding the difference between economic, political and social factors helps give structure to an answer to an 'Explain why' question. The chart that follows offers a list of reasons that are relevant to the answer to the question. Using the information on the opposite page and your own knowledge, decide whether each reason should be considered an economic, political or social factor and tick the appropriate box.

Explain why some Americans opposed immigration in the period 1890–1920.

	ECONOMIC	POLITICAL	SOCIAL
1. Immigrants such as the Slavic miners in Pennsylvania drove down wages and were used as strike-breakers.	✓		
2. Overcrowding and slum conditions, such as in New York, were often blamed on immigrants.			✓
3. The culture of some immigrant groups (e.g. Germans) involved alcohol which made them unpopular with temperance groups.			✓
4. Immigrants, such as the Italians, were blamed for taking the jobs of other Americans.	✓		✓
5. High crime rates were often blamed on immigrants and their gangs.			✓
6. The help given to immigrants in New York by Tammany Hall led to many immigrants voting for the Democrat Party and fuelled theories of Catholic conspiracies.		✓	
7. Many Americans believed that people from immigrant backgrounds, such as Emma Goldman, had extremist views.		✓	

Identify an argument

Below are a sample exam-style 24-mark question and two sample paragraphs. One suggests a high-level answer because it advances a supported argument. The other suggests a low-level answer because it contains only description and assertion. Identify which is which. The definitions below should help you:

- **Argument**: giving a view supported by reasoning and fact
- **Assertion**: giving a view that is not supported by reasoning and fact
- **Description**: providing facts but not in support of a view.

How far was anti-immigrant feeling in the period 1890–1920 mainly due to religious prejudice?

Paragraph 1

In the 1890s about 4 million immigrants came to the United States. Many of them were Italians, Jews, Russians and people from the Austro-Hungarian Empire. They often could not speak English and had different religious beliefs from many who already lived in the USA. Anti-immigrant groups did not like the immigrants who came from southern and eastern Europe and one of the things they objected to was the fact that a lot of them were Catholics or Jews.

Paragraph 2

One of the main reasons for anti-immigrant feeling during the period 1890–1920 seems to have been religious prejudice towards the 'new wave' of immigrants who had started to arrive in the USA by the end of the nineteenth century. Many 'new immigrants' from parts of southern and eastern Europe were Catholic or Jewish rather than Protestant. The animosity towards immigrants on religious grounds was well demonstrated by such nativist groups as the American Protective Association which opposed Catholic immigration, Catholic teachers in public (state) schools and Catholics holding any political office. The revival of the Ku Klux Klan post-First World War would see Catholics targeted once more.

The rise of big business and its impact on the economy

A number of factors influenced the rise of big business and the subsequent expansion of the economy in the USA in the late nineteenth and early twentieth centuries.

Raw materials and infrastructure

Economic and business growth would not have been possible without the abundance of raw materials in the USA:

- The vast areas of agricultural land provided the food needed to sustain the population and a surplus to sell abroad.
- The discovery of oilfields, such as Spindletop, Texas in 1901, and the anthracite coalfields of Pennsylvania proved crucial to industrial expansion providing the material for the mass production of steel.
- Between 1890 and 1913 US production of coal increased by 375 million tonnes and in the same period the production of iron ore by 22 million tonnes.

The growth of the railroads, under such businessmen as Cornelius Vanderbilt, provided a transport infrastructure which allowed new markets to be created.

Innovations

Innovations such as the Bessemer process adopted by Andrew Carnegie allowed for the mass production of cheaper steel. Additionally, the importance of electricity as a source of power became ever more apparent thanks to the efforts of men such as Thomas Edison and Nikola Tesla. Mass production techniques first used in 1914 by Henry Ford would be extremely significant in the longer term. They reduced the price not only of Ford cars, but also of all sorts of other products – in 1895 there were four cars in use in the USA, but by 1917 nearly 5 million were being driven.

Entrepreneurs

Famous entrepreneurs from the period include:

- Andrew Carnegie who dominated the steel industry
- John D. Rockefeller who set up Standard Oil
- J.P. Morgan who became so powerful in banking and finance that he played a major part in cutting deals which prevented economic disaster in 1907.

Attitudes of the federal government

The Republican Party in particular supported a *laissez-faire* approach to the economy. Nonetheless, from time to time certain presidents tried to clamp down on what they regarded as unfair **monopolies** which had reduced competition in the market. Unions received little sympathy from presidents, Congress or the Supreme Court during the period. The Republicans also favoured high tariffs which helped US manufacturers to undercut foreign competition. For example, the Dingley Tariff, introduced in 1897 under McKinley, was the highest tariff ever imposed and increased rates on a number of imported products.

Mass immigration and the weakness of unions

Despite the opposition to immigrants from some quarters, they provided a cheap unskilled workforce as well as a market for the goods produced. The US population grew by 40 million between 1890 and 1913 and this had a major impact on economic growth. It was difficult to form unions when so many workers were divided along ethnic and religious lines. John Mitchell's United Mine Workers had some success with strikes at the turn of the century in fighting low pay and poor conditions, but events such as the **Triangle Shirtwaist Fire** in 1911 in New York highlighted the terrible conditions in which many people worked on a daily basis. Other strikes such as Homestead Steel in 1892 and the Pullman Strike in 1894 were met with state-sanctioned violence which made it even more difficult for unions to make much headway.

! Make the links

Below are a sample exam-style 12-mark question and a series of relevant reasons that could be used in the answer. Read the question and add a comment and linking phrase to each reason to explain each reason and show how it relates to the following one.

Explain why the USA had become a major industrial power by 1914.

Reason	Comment and linking phrase leading to the next reason
Raw materials and infrastructure	Oil fields – Texas, lots of raw materials – 22 tonnes iron Steel etc.
Entrepreneurs and innovators	Edison + Tesla – Electricity. Carnegie – Bessemer process. – Rockefeller.
Attitudes of federal government	– Laissez Faire. – Bingley Tariff. – little sympathy for unions.

! Complete the paragraph

Below are a sample exam-style 24-mark question and the outline of a paragraph written in answer to this question. The paragraph begins with a relevant comment in relation to the question and ends with a further link. However, it lacks supporting examples. Complete the paragraph by providing some factual detail in the space provided.

How far was the economic success the USA had achieved by 1914 down to the initiatives of wealthy businessmen?

There can be little doubt that the actions and initiatives of a group of wealthy and powerful businessmen contributed greatly to the economic success of the USA in the late nineteenth and early twentieth centuries. For example …

_____

_____

_____

_____

_____

Consequently, due to the creation of large companies, innovative ideas and the adoption of modern techniques of production, certain wealthy businessmen were able to have a major impact on the economic success of the country.

Progressivism

Progressivism was a broad and diverse movement which emerged in the 1880s and 1890s as a response to the rapid rate of change at the end of the century and the inequalities of the post-Civil War period, although it was not until 1901 that the first Progressive president sat in the White House. The movement tended to support any measure that aimed to improve the lives of ordinary people, and encompassed campaigns to:

- ban alcohol
- reduce the power of big business and its leaders
- improve public health and food standards
- reduce crime
- enfranchise women
- improve working and living conditions
- protect the environment for future generations.

Three presidents took up Progressive causes before the impact of the First World War created a less idealistic outlook in the USA. The table below shows significant events during the terms of the 'Progressive presidents' – Roosevelt, Taft and Wilson.

Roosevelt, 1901–1909	
1901	Theodore Roosevelt (TR) began to use the 1891 Forest Reserve Act to protect 150 million acres of forest from big business during his presidency.
1902	TR intervened in a miners' strike on the side of the miners, resulting in a 10% pay increase and a nine-hour day.
1902	Newlands Act gave TR the power to allow land reclamation and dam building to help irrigation in the West.
1902	TR used the Sherman Act (1890) to dissolve J.P. Morgan's railroad holding company, Northern Securities.
1903	TR used an executive order to establish Pelican Island as the first national wildlife reserve to prevent birds being hunted for their feathers.
1906	Hepburn Railroad Regulation Act was passed. It permitted stricter regulation of the railroads and extended the powers of the ICC which had been passed to regulate interstate trade.
1906	Pure Food and Drug Act passed to regulate standards of products.
1906	Meat Inspection Act passed to regulate standards in the meat trade.
Taft, 1909–1913	
1909–1913	90 **anti-trust suits** were brought under Taft in four years compared to 44 under Roosevelt in eight years. Taft's prosecutions included the country's largest corporation, US Steel.
1910	Mann–Elkins Act further extended the scope of the ICC.
1910	Taft established El Dorado National Forest in California.
1910	General Withdrawal Act, which was used by Taft to withdraw 8.5 million acres of land in Alaska from the public domain to stop private companies buying them up.
1912	Federal Children's Bureau created to clamp down on child abuse.
Wilson, 1913–1921	
1913	Wilson used patronage to pass the Underwood–Simmons Tariff Act which cut duties and publicly denounced corporate lobbyists.
1914	Clayton Anti-Trust Act passed to combat monopolies; made individuals responsible if their companies broke the law.
1916	Federal Farm Loan Act helped to provide cheaper mortgages for farmers.
1916	Adamson Act imposed an eight-hour day at the same pay for railroad workers.
1917–1918	Espionage, Sabotage and Sedition Acts, which all curtailed the civil liberties of Americans in the name of national security, and resulted in the arrest of thousands who had opposed the war.
1919	Nineteenth Amendment passed giving women the vote.

Complete the paragraph

Below are a sample exam-style 24-mark question and the outline of a paragraph written in answer to this question. The paragraph begins with a relevant comment in relation to the question and ends with a further link. However, it lacks supporting examples. Complete the paragraph by providing some factual detail in the space provided.

How successful were the Progressive reforms of Presidents Roosevelt, Taft and Wilson in improving the lives of American people between 1901 and 1921?

One of the ways in which the Progressive presidents aimed to improve the lives of the American people was to protect them from the monopolistic practices and powerful influence of the leaders of big business.

_____

_____

_____

_____

The results of Progressive reform in terms of improving prices and choice for the consumer were therefore limited, although reforms did attempt to deal with the worst cases of monopolistic practice.

Develop the detail

Below are a sample exam-style 24-mark question and a paragraph written in answer to this. The paragraph contains a limited amount of detail. Annotate the paragraph to add additional detail to the answer.

How far is it true to say that Theodore Roosevelt proved to be a more Progressive President than Taft or Wilson?

It can be argued in terms of their attitudes towards the power of big business that Theodore Roosevelt was not as Progressive as Taft or Wilson. Roosevelt intervened on the side of the workers in the miners' strike of 1902. He also brought a lot of land under government protection to stop it being exploited by big business, and used a law to dissolve a railroad company and other trusts. A lot more trusts, however, were prosecuted when Taft was president including the biggest corporation in the country, and Taft also brought more land under his protection. Wilson actually improved on the laws which investigated the trusts and introduced a shorter working day for railroad workers. It could be argued that he achieved more in this area than Roosevelt too.

US foreign policy, 1890–c1913

Timeline of key events in US foreign policy, 1890–1913

This period saw increasing US involvement in the Americas and Caribbean and also in South East Asia and the Pacific.

- 1894 US troops sent to Nicaragua following a revolution there, to protect US interests
- 1898
  - April–August – Spanish-American War fought in Cuba and the Philippines
  - July – US annexation of Hawaii
  - December – USA took control of Puerto Rico, Guam and the Philippines by the terms of the Treaty of Paris
- 1899 **Open Door policy** regarding China announced to permit the USA to trade there alongside other countries
- 1900 Boxer rebellion in China against western influence brought US intervention
- 1902 Platt Amendment confirmed US influence over Cuba
- 1904 Roosevelt Corollary to the Monroe Doctrine implied that the USA could interfere in the Americas where it felt its own interests were at stake
- 1906 Panama Canal project started by Theodore Roosevelt (finished 1914)

The influences on US foreign policy in the period 1890–c1920

Economic influences

Former naval commander Alfred Mahan argued in 1890 that naval expansion was needed to support economic expansion.

Senator Henry Cabot Lodge wrote about expanding US influence to safeguard commercial interest and to avoid the 1893 panic happening again.

Following the Spanish-American War, which had been backed by many business leaders, by the 1920s 75 per cent of Cuban imports came from the USA, and 80 per cent of Cuban exports went to the USA.

Presidential influence

McKinley believed that an active foreign policy would aid economic recovery and help him get re-elected in 1900, hence US involvement in Cuba (when Spain refused to give up control of the island) and the Boxer Rebellion in China.

Theodore Roosevelt tended to prioritise prestige and security. As president he was behind the building of the Panama Canal and the expansion of the US Navy which improved the security of the USA, but did not take the USA into any new wars. He acted as a mediator in the 1905 negotiations between Russia and Japan, for which he won the Nobel Peace prize.

Taft preferred '**dollar diplomacy**'. Nonetheless, he sent marines to Nicaragua to protect the banking house of Brown Brothers.

Imperialistic and anti-imperialistic thinking

In 1898 the USA gained control over Puerto Rico, Guam, the Philippines and Hawaii. The Platt Amendment gave the USA a certain amount of control over Cuba.

The war of 1898 was presented as a crusade against imperial Spain, and the USA had not forgotten its own former colonial status.

The Anti-Imperialist League backed by Andrew Carnegie put pressure on presidents to avoid hostilities abroad.

Public opinion

The '**Yellow Press**' of William Hearst (*New York Journal*) and Pulitzer (*New York World*) sensationalised Spanish atrocities in Cuba, and blamed the sinking of the *USS Maine,* in Havana Harbour in February 1898, on the Spanish. A leaked letter written by Spanish ambassador de Lôme which insulted McKinley was also well covered in the *New York Journal*. Public opinion in turn was affected by the press.

Incidents and events outside US control

In the build-up to the Spanish-American War the harsh Spanish treatment of Cubans in the 1890s and the cruelties of General 'Butcher' Weyler influenced American opinion, as did the explosion of the *Maine*.

Ideological/humanitarian factors

McKinley said that it was 'a duty ... to civilisation and humanity, to intervene with force' regarding Cuba and many Americans supported this apparently moral stance.

Prioritisation

Below are a sample exam-style 12-mark question and a list of reasons that could be used in the answer. Demonstrating prioritisation is one way of structuring the answer to an 'Explain why' question. Using your own knowledge and the information on the opposite page, decide the order of priority you would give to these factors. Write numbers on the spectrum below to indicate their relative importance and, beneath each, briefly justify that factor's placement, demonstrating why you feel some factors are more important than others.

Explain why the USA went to war with the Spanish in 1898.

1. Role of the 'Yellow Press' in stirring up public opinion
2. Public opinion which was outraged by the tales of 'Butcher' Weyler
3. A number of business leaders favoured war on the grounds that Cuba and the Philippines might help to revive the economy
4. McKinley's role regarding his ideological reasons, his concerns about the economy, his desire to be re-elected in 1900, and his reaction to Spain's refusal to give up control of Cuba
5. The explosion of the *USS Maine* in Havana Harbour
6. The letter written by Spanish minister de Lôme which insulted McKinley and was published in the *New York Journal*

Most important					Least important
3	1	5	2	4	6

Turning assertion into argument   (a)

Below are a sample exam-style 24-mark question and a series of assertions. Read the question and then add a justification to each of the assertions to turn it into a supported view, so creating an argument.

How important was Theodore Roosevelt in the development of US foreign policy in the years 1897–1913?

Roosevelt was important to the development of US foreign policy because ...

Panama, U.S. navy, meditraiber m/reos.

Taft was important to the development of US foreign policy because ...

Dollar Diplomacy, marony to Nocaricqua.

McKinley was also important to the development of US foreign policy because ...

Spanish · American war, Open Door

Woodrow Wilson's foreign policy, 1913–1921

It is sometimes assumed that Wilson's approach to foreign policy was more ethical, more peaceful, less interventionist and less imperialistic than the foreign policies of McKinley, Roosevelt and Taft. However, the evidence does not necessarily suggest that this was the case. Wilson's foreign policy interests can be broken down into three main areas.

The First World War and Europe

Wilson's position on the First World War changed over time. As early as 1914 Wilson had admitted 'England is fighting our fight'. However, Wilson continued to maintain an official policy of neutrality despite press coverage of German wartime atrocities in Belgium and the German sinking of the *Lusitania* in May 1915. Notably, many German Americans and Irish Americans (who disapproved of British policy in Ireland) were against the USA helping the British. The press was also divided on the issue. For example, journalist William Hearst took an anti-British line. During the 1916 election campaign Wilson remained pledged to neutrality. Following the German resumption of unrestricted submarine warfare in January 1917 and the publication of the Zimmermann Telegram in February 1917, which revealed a German attempt to back a Mexican invasion of the USA, Wilson committed the USA to war in April 1917. By that stage US bankers had lent the Allies $2.5 billion but only $27 million to the **Central Powers**, and the country could simply not afford to let the Allies lose the war.

Wilson's decision to enter the war in 1917 also gave him the chance to play a major role at the Paris Peace Conference at the end of the war. His 'Fourteen Points' proposal would form the basis for negotiations which resulted in the Treaty of Versailles, and led to the setting up of the League of Nations. Senator Henry Cabot Lodge, however, spoke out against the League of Nations on the grounds that membership might endanger the existence of the USA by involving it in unnecessary wars, and the Senate voted against US membership of the League and the Versailles Treaty.

Despite his belief in self-determination – that peoples of the world should be free to decide their own form of government – Wilson sent US troops to Russia where they ended up fighting the Bolsheviks in 1918.

The Americas and the Caribbean

Following General Huerta's overthrow of the Mexican government in 1913, Wilson sent in US troops to protect American business interests in Mexico, *and* when Pancho Villa staged a second revolution. Wilson massed 100,000 troops on the Texas border for invasion in 1916 when it looked as if American interests might be in danger. Mediation saved the day, however, and a treaty was signed in January 1917.

Wilson also sent US troops to occupy Nicaragua, Haiti and the Dominican Republic in 1914, 1915 and 1916 respectively to protect American interests, abandoning his ideas for self-determination. In the Caribbean he also bought the Danish West Indies to stop them falling into German hands in 1916, and they were renamed the Virgin Islands.

South East Asia and the Pacific

Wilson backed the Jones Act of 1916 which gave the Filipinos more autonomy. He also backed the Open Door policy regarding China. Wilson's recognition of the new Chinese republican government, established in 1911, improved relations with China. However, US relations with Japan worsened as the Japanese wanted to gain territory in China. In 1915 the USA was unhappy with the Japanese rejection of the Open Door policy. Wilson's Secretary of State William Jennings Bryan expressed concern regarding further Japanese encroachments in China. Nonetheless, he recognised Japan's 'special interests' in Manchuria, Mongolia and Shandong. The Lansing-Ishii agreement was signed in 1917 and formalised this US understanding with Japan.

Prioritisation

Below are a sample exam-style 12-mark question and a list of reasons that could be used in the answer. Demonstrating prioritisation is one way of structuring the answer to an 'Explain why' question. Using your own knowledge and the information on the opposite page, decide the order of priority you would give to these factors. Write numbers on the spectrum below to indicate their relative importance and, beneath each, briefly justify that factor's placement, demonstrating why you feel some factors are more important than others.

Explain why the USA entered the First World War in 1917.

1. Press coverage of German atrocities in Belgium
2. The sinking of the *Lusitania*
3. US bankers had lent far more money to the Allies than to the Central Powers and could not afford to let Britain and France lose the war
4. Entering the war gave Wilson an opportunity to have a major influence on the post-war peace settlements
5. The German declaration that they were restarting unrestricted submarine warfare in January 1917
6. The revelation of the Zimmermann Telegram which encouraged the Mexicans to invade the USA

Most important   Least important

6	1	2	5	3	*Would've entered it but was earlier it was 'case*

You're the examiner

Below are a sample exam-style 24-mark question and a paragraph written in answer to this question. Read the paragraph and the mark scheme provided on page 3. Decide which level you would award the paragraph. Write the level below, along with a justification for your decision.

How far was German aggression the main reason for the entry of the USA into the First World War in 1917?

It can be argued that German aggression was a major reason for US intervention in the First World War, although it should be pointed out that the German sinking of the Lusitania with the loss of 128 lives took place in May 1915, nearly two years before Wilson committed the USA to war in April of 1917. This would suggest that this earlier phase of German U-boat attacks on 'neutral' shipping was not what provoked the USA into war. The fact that Wilson went into the 1916 election campaign pledging to stay out of the war also suggests that his reasons for declaring war came after November 1916. It does seem, however, that the German decision to renew unrestricted submarine warfare in January 1917 quickly followed in February by the revelation of the Zimmermann Telegram, which aimed to support a Mexican invasion of the USA, were the crucial factors in Wilson's decision to go to war. It could, however, be counter-argued that these German actions merely gave the USA the excuse to intervene in a war it could not afford to let the Allies lose.

develops debate

Level: _____ Reason for choosing this level: _____

_____

_____

The introduction of Prohibition

In January 1919 the Eighteenth Amendment was ratified banning the manufacture, sale and transportation of alcohol across the USA. In October 1919 the **Volstead Act,** also known as the National Prohibition Act, was passed which contained the legislative detail for the enforcement of the amendment.

Why was Prohibition introduced?

Campaign groups

Campaign groups such as the Women's Christian Temperance Union (WCTU) set up in 1874 had helped to establish that alcohol had harmful effects on society. They succeeded in gaining the prohibition of alcohol at a local level in states such as Kansas, but by the 1890s had made little impact nationally.

In 1893, however, the Anti-Saloon League (ASL) was set up by Protestant businessmen in Ohio. The ASL aimed to achieve a national ban: the complete prohibition of alcohol across the whole country. Wayne Wheeler became legal adviser to the ASL and used its funds to back 'dry' political candidates of either party. Wheeler's influence can be seen in his prevention of the re-election of Ohio state governor Myron T. Herrick in 1906. Wheeler, who based himself in Washington, D.C., put more pressure on politicians. He realised that the 1920 census would show that a majority of US citizens lived in largely **'wet'** urban areas and the numbers in the House of Representatives would be reapportioned to reflect this. This in turn would reduce the chances of a Prohibition amendment gaining the two-thirds majority it needed. Wheeler's influence was such that it was claimed he actually drafted the Volstead Act.

Individual states banning alcohol

The campaign in favour of Prohibition was helped by the fact that by 1912 half the states had gone dry, and in 1913 the Webb–Kenyon Act forbade the transport of liquor from wet to dry states.

Anti-immigrant feeling

One of the reasons many Americans disapproved of immigrants was because of the prevalent drinking culture of Irish, German and Jewish communities.

This anti-immigrant feeling was often linked to support for Prohibition.

Attitudes of industrialists

Businessmen such as Henry Ford supported and funded Prohibition campaigning because he felt that alcohol undermined the efficiency of his workers, and if people were spending money on alcohol they would not be able to afford his cars.

Failure of brewers and distillers to unite

Brewers argued that beer was healthy and turned on distillers, claiming that spirits were harmful, in the hope that they could deflect criticism from themselves. This prevented them joining together to put forward a united front against Prohibition.

Introduction of income tax

The Sixteenth Amendment of 1913, which allowed the federal government to levy income tax, removed a major obstacle to Prohibition. As much as 70 per cent of internal government revenue had come from alcohol in some years, and there could clearly be no Prohibition amendment until government had found an alternative source of revenue. The ASL campaigned to get this amendment through.

The First World War

Whisky was considered a waste of grain during wartime, and Congress banned the use of grain for making spirits. Uniformed men were barred from saloons. Anti-German feeling grew during the war as sympathy for the Allies increased, and as most brewers in the USA came from German backgrounds, such as Adolphus Busch, beer was referred to as 'Kaiser Brew' and seen as unpatriotic. The US entry into the war created enough support in Congress to pass the Prohibition amendment. At Wheeler's instigation, the Senate investigated the links between the brewers and the National German-American Alliance (NGAA), which led to the NGAA folding in April 1918. The NGAA favoured US neutrality, had raised money for war relief in Germany, and was strongly opposed to Prohibition. The war provided the final push for the Prohibition amendment to be passed and ratified.

Long-term or short-term?

Below is a sample exam-style 12-mark question which asks for a range of reasons. Understanding the difference between long-term and short-term factors helps give structure to an answer to an 'Explain why' question. The chart that follows offers a list of reasons that are relevant to the answer to the question. Using the information on the opposite page and your own knowledge, decide whether each reason should be considered a long- or short-term factor and tick the appropriate box.

Explain why the Prohibition amendment was added to the Constitution.

	LONG-TERM	SHORT-TERM
1. The work of campaign groups		
2. Individual states imposing bans on alcohol		
3. Anti-immigrant feeling		
4. Industrialists' opposition to drink		
5. The introduction of income tax		
6. The impact of the First World War		

Turning assertion into argument

Below are a sample exam-style 24-mark question and a series of assertions. Read the question and then add a justification to each of the assertions to turn it into a supported view, so creating an argument.

How far was the ratification of the Prohibition amendment down to the work of the Anti-Saloon League?

The ratification of the Prohibition amendment was a result of the pressure which the Anti-Saloon League put on politicians of both major parties ...

_____

_____

The ratification of the Prohibition amendment came about as a result of the First World War making drinking alcohol seem unpatriotic ...

_____

_____

The ratification of the Prohibition amendment happened because American industrialists wanted to stop their workers drinking ...

_____

_____

Exam focus

Below is a sample A-grade answer for a 12-mark question. Read the brief plan, the answer and the examiner's comments around it.

Explain why the Prohibition amendment was added to the US Constitution in 1919.

The plan identifies three factors which should aid the structure of the answer.

There is direct reference to what the question asks which is an effective way to begin an answer.

This paragraph suggests that the First World War was the most important short-term reason and provides evidence to support this view, as well as suggesting that the war had a double impact. This demonstrates prioritisation of causes and the ability to differentiate between longer- and shorter-term causation, which are impressive 'Level 4 skills'.

This paragraph provides a second factor with links to the war mentioned in the first paragraph, as well as going into good detail and showing a good understanding of how an amendment is achieved. Linkage of factors and good supporting detail will help an answer get into Level 4 of the mark scheme.

Plan:
- The impact of the First World War
- Campaigning groups, especially the Anti-Saloon League
- The importance of the Sixteenth Amendment

It can be argued that the most important short-term cause of the Prohibition amendment was the impact of the First World War. The war unleashed anti-German feeling in the country which had a huge significance because most of the breweries in the USA were owned by German-Americans such as Adolphus Busch. The USA's entry into the war in 1917 also emphasised the importance of food production over alcohol, which helped to persuade many that alcohol production should be limited or banned. Once the war started the NGAA (National German-American Alliance) supported neutrality and raised money to send to Germany for war relief, and this gave supporters of Prohibition the ideal opportunity to depict any supporters of alcohol as un-American, pro-German, food-wasting and generally disloyal to the USA. Beer was referred to as 'Kaiser Brew' and the USA's entry into the war tipped the numbers needed in Congress to achieve the two-thirds majority needed for an amendment.

The First World War would not, however, have had the massive impact it did without the longer-term campaigning of such groups as the Women's Christian Temperance Union (WCTU), which had helped to establish the arguments against alcohol in many parts of the country, although by the 1890s, the WCTU had failed to have much impact nationally. In 1893, however, the Anti-Saloon League was set up and immediately set about trying to put pressure on individual politicians from both main parties to support Prohibition. Wayne Wheeler became the leading figure of the League and set up an office in Washington, D.C. from where he could put greater pressure on members of Congress. With the opportunities provided by the war, the League continued to press its aims in the hope that an amendment might be passed before the 1920 census brought about a reapportionment of numbers in the House of Representatives and gave a majority to those from urban areas, who would be less in favour of Prohibition. It is claimed that the Volstead Act, which dealt with the details of Prohibition enforcement, was actually drafted by Wayne Wheeler, which demonstrates further the influence the Anti-Saloon League had.

The role of the Anti-Saloon League is also linked to a third reason behind the Prohibition amendment, which was the Sixteenth Amendment to the Constitution, ratified in 1913. Wheeler had campaigned for this amendment which established the government's power to levy income tax. Before this time as much as 70 per cent of internal government revenue had come from alcohol, and there could clearly be no Prohibition amendment until the government had found an alternative source of revenue. The Sixteenth Amendment clearly removed an obstacle to Prohibition before the impact of the First World War, and although it can be argued that the war had a double impact on the success of the Prohibition campaign, the work of Wayne Wheeler and the Anti-Saloon League had elevated the campaign to a national level, and should probably be regarded as the crucial factor in the ratification of the Eighteenth Amendment.

This final paragraph has linkage to the Anti-Saloon League covered in the second paragraph and provides a different sort of factor. It also contains a concluding sentence which draws together the three factors in order to reach a final decision on which is the most important factor. This again demonstrates the ability to prioritise.

12/12

The answer offers three different and well-linked reasons. It is impressive because of the amount of precise detail it conveys and the structured way in which the factors are presented. It shows a very high level of understanding and so gains full marks.

Identifying links in a 12-mark answer

This response shows a high-level answer to an 'Explain why' question which reaches the top mark because it contains some impressive links between the factors it advances. Go through the answer and make a list of those links. Consider how these links are incorporated into the answer.

Section 2:
The USA, c1920–1929

Post-war attitudes and the Red Scare

During the First World War a xenophobic mood swept the country, and following the war Americans seemed to want to turn away from the problems of the wider world. The success of the **Bolshevik Revolution** in Russia in 1917 and the establishment of the Soviet Union convinced many Americans that communists, anarchists and socialists in the USA would attempt to inspire the workers to bring down the US government. The Red Scare was the term given to such fears in the immediate post-war period. The factors that led to the Red Scare are outlined below.

Immigration

Many Americans had been concerned about the changing nature of immigration since the late nineteenth century and felt suspicious of those coming from southern and eastern Europe. Violence such as Polish-American Leon Czolgosz's assassination of President McKinley in 1901 created a fear of anarchism, and linked it to European immigrants. Following a payroll robbery in April 1920 in which two men were killed, people were only too willing to believe that two Italian anarchist immigrants, Sacco and Vanzetti, were guilty.

First World War

The patriotism of the war also contributed to an atmosphere where foreigners and anyone with left-wing views were distrusted and suspected of disloyalty. During the war the leader of the Socialist Labour Party, Eugene Debs, was arrested. German-Jewish immigrant Robert Goldstein who produced the film *The Spirit of '76*, which portrayed British atrocities during the American Revolution, was initially jailed for ten years because his film created ill-feeling towards the British, who were wartime allies.

The Russian Revolution

The success of the Russian Bolshevik Party in overthrowing the Russian government in October 1917 in the name of the workers was a key factor leading to the Red Scare. The Bolshevik emphasis on **World Revolution** (plus subsequent uprisings in Germany and Hungary in 1919) persuaded many that American workers might plan a similar uprising.

Rise in the number of strikes

A wave of strikes hit the country after the war, which included a general strike centred on Seattle in February 1919 and a strike of the entire Boston police force in September 1919. The strikes focused on pay, conditions and hours, and the impact of the post-war slump, and were not politically motivated. The press, however, linked them to left-wing conspiracies and dubbed the strikers 'reds'.

Bombings

In April 1919, 36 mail bombs were discovered which were to be delivered on 1 May. One of the bombs was to be sent to Attorney General A. Mitchell Palmer. In June 1919 Palmer's Washington house was bombed, and in September 1920 an explosion on Wall Street killed 31 people and injured hundreds. All of these incidents were attributed to anarchist groups and helped to fuel the Red Scare.

The Palmer Raids

Mitchell Palmer's Raids, which began in November 1919 and aimed to arrest anyone suspected of plotting against the state, were a response to the bomb threats and the wider Red Scare, and possibly an attempt by Palmer to establish himself as a potential presidential candidate. The raids led to arrests (about 10,000) and deportations which increased people's suspicions of foreigners and immigrants. Palmer's predictions of more violence in May 1920 came to nothing and the Red Scare petered out, along with his political ambitions.

Make the links

Below are a sample exam-style 12-mark question and a series of relevant reasons that could be used in the answer. Read the question and add a comment and linking phrase to each reason to explain each reason and show how it relates to the following one.

Explain why the Palmer Raids took place in the winter of 1919–1920.

Reason	Comment and linking phrase leading to the next reason
Fears of anarchism and communism had become greater since the assassination of President McKinley and the Russian Revolution of 1917.	
A number of mail bombs were sent in April/May 1919, including one which exploded at the house of Attorney General Palmer.	
Palmer harboured ambitions of running for president and it could be argued that thousands of arrests and deportations would go down well with the public.	

Specific or underlying?

Below is a sample exam-style 12-mark question, which asks for a range of reasons. Understanding the difference between specific and more general or 'underlying' reasons helps give structure to an answer to an 'Explain why' question. The chart that follows offers a list of reasons that are relevant to the answer to this question. Using the information on the previous page and your own knowledge, decide whether each reason should be considered a specific or underlying factor and tick the appropriate box.

Explain why the Red Scare took place in the USA in 1919–1920.

	UNDERLYING	SPECIFIC
1. Fear of anarchism, communism and socialism	✓	
2. The Russian Revolution		✓
3. Bombings		✓
4. First World War	✓	
5. Immigrants coming from eastern and southern Europe	✓	
6. Strikes of 1919		✓

The rise of the Ku Klux Klan

What was the Ku Klux Klan?

The Ku Klux Klan (KKK), which had originally existed for a short period after the American Civil War (1861–1865), was re-founded by William Simmons in 1915. Members of the 'new' Klan were worried about Catholic and Jewish influence in the USA, the rising prominence of black Americans, and the apparent decline of morality in the USA. By 1925 the organisation had around 4 million members.

Underlying attitudes and events which created sympathy for the Klan

Anti-immigrant attitudes

As we have seen on pages 8–22 the nature of immigration changed in the late nineteenth century. Immigrants from eastern Europe began to be perceived as a threat by some **WASP** Americans and **nativist** groups. Concerns about immigrants included:

- their growing political influence and perceived corruption (e.g. Tammany Hall, see page 8)
- their willingness to work for low wages and the concern that this kept wages down for all
- whether they were loyal to the USA (e.g. during the First World War)
- their links to Communism in the wake of the Bolshevik Revolution in 1917
- their association with a drinking culture and willingness to flout Prohibition legislation in the 1920s, which made them a threat to law and order
- their links to the Red Scare of 1919–1920 (see page 22).

Anti-black attitudes

Between 1900 and 1910 around 2 million black Americans left the South for northern cities such as Detroit, where they competed for jobs with white Americans and immigrants. Black men who had fought during the First World War were less likely to accept white supremacy when they returned. The race riot in Chicago in 1919, where 38 died, highlights these tensions.

Anti-modern attitudes

Many Americans were wary of the growth of cities and associated them with modern ideas which undermined morality. In the 1920s more women went to work, smoked and drank, and wore shorter skirts. The idea of the 'new woman' worried those who believed in more traditional roles for the sexes.

How the Klan increased its support

Exploitation of anti-immigrant fears

The Klan spread hysterical fears about papal control of America and campaigned against Catholic Al Smith, the Democratic candidate in the 1928 presidential elections. **Anti-Semitic** newspapers such as Henry Ford's *Dearborn Independent* compounded the prejudice.

Exploiting publicity

In 1921 the *New York World* ran an exposé of the Klan and a Congressional investigation looked into allegations of financial irregularities and atrocities, unwittingly providing the Klan with much publicity. Simmons later said: 'Congress made us'.

'Birth of a Nation'

D.W. Griffith's film *Birth of a Nation* released in 1915 glorified the post-Civil War Klan and helped recruitment to Simmons' organisation in the early days.

Ritual

The use of burning crosses, hooded costumes and mysterious names for ceremonies and meetings all seemed to appeal to a 'small town' mentality in search of excitement.

Links to religion/morality

At its peak the KKK had half a million female members. This may have been a result of the Klan linking itself to churches, especially in rural areas, and supporting such ideas as 'the purity of white womanhood' and women voting, which the KKK felt would help to restore traditional morality.

Use of professional promoters

Professional promoters Elizabeth Tyler and Edward Y. Clarke brought modern techniques to Klan propaganda, such as promoting a Klan newspaper, to give it a broader appeal.

Long-term or short-term?

Below is a sample exam-style 12-mark question, which asks for a range of reasons. Understanding the difference between long-term and short-term factors helps give structure to an answer to an 'Explain why' question. The chart that follows offers a list of reasons that are relevant to the answer to this question. Using the information on the opposite page and your own knowledge, decide whether each reason should be considered a long- or short-term factor and tick the appropriate box.

Explain why the Ku Klux Klan attracted so many members in the USA in the 1920s.

	LONG-TERM	SHORT-TERM
1. Anti-immigrant feeling	✓	
2. Professional promoters Tyler and Clarke		✓
3. Anti-black feeling	✓	
4. Red Scare	✓	
5. Publicity		✓
6. *Birth of a Nation* film		✓

Identify an argument

Below are a sample exam-style 24-mark question and two sample paragraphs. One suggests a high-level answer because it advances supported arguments and contains some balance. The other suggests a low-level answer because it contains only description and assertion. Identify which is which. The definitions below should help you:

- **Argument**: giving a view supported by reasoning and detailed evidence
- **Assertion**: stating a view which is not supported by reasoning and evidence
- **Description**: providing facts which do not support a view.

How far can the rise of the Ku Klux Klan in the 1920s be put down to anti-immigrant feeling?

Paragraph 1

The Ku Klux Klan disliked Jews, Catholics, black people and immigrants, and members liked the burning crosses, hooded costumes and ceremonies which had been dreamt up by William Simmons who re-founded the Klan in 1915 during the First World War. It is believed that by 1925 the Klan may have had as many as 4 million members.

Paragraph 2

Anti-immigrant feeling towards certain groups in the USA undoubtedly had a big impact on the rise of the Ku Klux Klan in 1920s America, although other factors may also need to be considered, such as prejudice towards black Americans and fears about declining moral standards, particularly in the growing cities. The years prior to the First World War had seen a large growth in the number of Catholic and Jewish immigrants coming from eastern Europe, while the war itself had exacerbated anti-immigrant feeling, and the Bolshevik Revolution had in turn created a fear that immigrants from eastern Europe had communist sympathies.

The reasons for the economic boom of the 1920s

During the 1920s the USA experienced an economic boom. The main reasons for this were as follows:

The impact of the First World War

The expansion of mass production techniques and the profits made by companies producing war-related products underpinned the growth of the 1920s. US Steel's profits more than doubled during the war years, and General Motors' yearly profits trebled to nearly $22 million. The USA's position as a creditor nation after the war allowed it to take advantage of debtor nations in terms of trade.

Mass production, entrepreneurs and raw materials

Scientific management known as 'Taylorism' and mass production techniques had a big impact on productivity. In 1929, 10 million radio sets were made (compared with 60,000 in 1920) and 5.5 million cars. Entrepreneur Henry Ford had set up the first moving assembly line in 1913 in Detroit. He was selling a basic Model T car for $950 in 1914, but by 1929 one cost just $290. Cars led to the expansion of cities by allowing people to live in suburbs, as well as enabling them to travel to the cinema, which in turn stimulated the movie industry. In 1922 movie theatres were selling 40 million tickets a week, rising to 100 million by 1929.

Car production depended greatly on the abundance of raw materials in the USA. It used up:

- 75 per cent of glass produced in the USA
- 96 per cent of its oil
- 65 per cent of its leather
- 80 per cent of its rubber
- 20 per cent of its steel.

Policies of Republican presidents

Presidents Warren Harding (1921–1923) and Calvin Coolidge (1923–1929) essentially adopted a **laissez-faire** approach to the economy, not particularly regulating the stock market, and allowing the market to set prices and wages, but they did intervene in the economy when necessary. For example, the Federal Aid Highway Act of 1921 helped to set up a national highway system of roads, with more than $75 million being spent within a year, which helped to sustain car production. Harding also supported the Fordney–McCumber tariff of 1922, which made imported food more expensive in order to help American farmers to sell their produce and to keep money inside the USA.

The tendency of Republican administrations not to prosecute **monopolies** allowed businessmen, such as Samuel Insull of General Electric, a freer hand to build on their wartime profits. Harding and Coolidge also allowed the expansion of credit and bank lending, and pursued a peaceful foreign policy which aimed to secure overseas markets. Andrew Mellon, Secretary of the Treasury 1921–1932, facilitated cuts in tax rates for the rich (from 50 per cent to 25 per cent) and poor (from 4 per cent to 3 per cent), which left them with more to spend or invest.

Expansion of credit and customer demand

Customer demand went up in the 1920s as wages rose, prices dropped, and credit became more easily available. In 1929, 80 per cent of radios were bought on credit as well as 60 per cent of the 26 million cars sold. Average industrial wages went up by about $5 a week during the decade, which fuelled the consumer boom.

Weakness of unions

Employers, the government and the courts which backed '**yellow dog**' no-strike contracts helped to keep unions relatively weak and stop wages from rising as quickly as they might have done. This allowed producers to keep prices relatively low.

Make the links

Below are a sample exam-style 12-mark question and a series of relevant reasons that could be used in the answer. Read the question and add a comment and linking phrase to each reason to explain each reason and show how it relates to the following one.

Explain why there was an economic boom in the USA in the 1920s.

Reason	Comment and linking phrase leading to the next reason
Assembly line production	
Manufacture of cars	
Federal road building	

Eliminate irrelevance

Below are a sample exam-style 24-mark question and a paragraph written in answer to it. Read the paragraph and identify parts that are not directly relevant or helpful to the question. Draw a line through the information that is irrelevant and justify your reasons in the margin.

How far was the role of entrepreneurial businessmen the main reason for the economic boom of the 1920s?

Henry Ford was one of the businessmen who had a huge impact on the economic boom of the 1920s. Henry Ford set up the first moving assembly line in 1913 in Detroit and became famous for building the Model T car. By 1929 one cost as little as $290. Car production had big knock-on effects as 75 per cent of the glass made in the USA and 96 per cent of the oil produced were used by the car industry. Samuel Insull of General Electric was another entrepreneur who took advantage of the lax regulation of business during the decade to dominate the electricity industry. Such men as Ford and Insull played a huge part in the economic boom of the 1920s.

The ending of mass immigration

The First World War seemed to bring fears about immigration to a head as the loyalty of ethnic groups that had originated in Germany or the Austro-Hungarian Empire was called into question. The Bolshevik Revolution of 1917 and the subsequent Red Scare (see page 22) after the war led to even greater fears that many of the people coming into the USA did not share the same political, social and religious values as most of the people who already lived there.

A number of Acts were passed to try to limit immigration. Their terms were influenced by the Immigration Restriction League, which had long campaigned to limit immigration, particularly from southern and eastern Europe and Asia.

Immigration Act, 1917

This Act raised the price of entry for immigrants and extended categories of those to be denied entry (on the grounds that they might become an economic burden to the country) to include homosexuals, criminals, epileptics, insane persons, alcoholics, polygamists and anarchists. It also barred immigrants over the age of sixteen who could not read 30–80 words in any language, and in addition it designated an **'Asiatic Barred Zone'**, from which no people could emigrate to the USA. Such was the support for the bill in Congress that President Wilson's (1913–1921) **veto** was overridden.

The Emergency Quota Act, 1921

In order to reduce unemployment at a time of economic recession (GNP dropped by about 10 per cent during 1920–1921 and unemployment rose by nearly 5 million) the Emergency Quota Act was introduced as a temporary measure. The Act:

■ set an overall limit of 357,000 immigrants a year
■ fixed quotas for national groups based on 3 per cent of the number of foreign-born residents from those groups who lived in the USA at the time of the 1910 census.

Johnson–Reed Act (National Origins Act), 1924

The Johnson–Reed Act provided for permanent legislation and aimed to significantly reduce the number of southern and eastern Europeans being allowed into the country. It also excluded Asians completely on the grounds that people from countries such as Japan, China and the Philippines were not eligible to be **naturalised** according to an Act of 1790 which stated that non-white immigrants could not be naturalised. No limits were set on immigrants from Latin American countries whose cheap labour was vital to farming in California.

Quotas were fixed at 2 per cent of those groups living in the USA in 1890 which massively reduced mass immigration from eastern and southern Europe. Senator Reed, who gave his name to the 1924 Act, had spoken of the need to keep American 'stock' up to the highest standard and to exclude the sick and the starving from southern and eastern Europe who were not able to adapt to American culture. Many supporters of the bill were **eugenicists** who believed that northern European races were superior, although Samuel Gompers, the Jewish founder of the AFL union, favoured the Act because immigrants increased competition for jobs and drove down wages.

When the Act came into force in 1929 the annual limit was set at 150,000 immigrants, and about 85 per cent of that figure was allocated to people from western and northern Europe with Germany, Britain and Ireland given the highest quotas. Immigration from Italy fell by more than 90 per cent following the Act, from around 200,000 per year before the war to about 4000 per year.

Prioritisation

Below are a sample exam-style 12-mark question and a list of reasons that could be used in the answer. Demonstrating prioritisation is one way of structuring the answer to an 'Explain why' question. Using your own knowledge and the information on the opposite page (and from earlier in Section 2), decide the order of priority you would give to these factors. Write numbers on the spectrum below to indicate their relative importance and, beneath each, briefly justify that factor's placement, demonstrating why you feel some factors are more important than others.

> Explain why immigration restriction Acts were passed by Congress during the early 1920s.

1. Anti-foreign feeling stirred up by the First World War and the Russian Revolution
2. Internal problems such as the Red Scare
3. The belief that some immigrants would be an economic burden on American society
4. The feeling that some immigrants were unable to adapt to American culture
5. The belief among many that certain races were inferior to WASPs
6. Immigrants drove down wages

Most important					Least important
1	2	5	4	3	6

 Develop the detail **a**

Below are a sample exam-style 24 mark question and a paragraph written in answer to this. The paragraph contains a limited amount of detail. Annotate the paragraph to add additional detail to the answer.

> How far were the immigration Acts passed by Congress in the 1920s essentially aimed at reducing immigration from southern and eastern Europe and Asia?

It can be argued that the USA before 1890 had been made up essentially of people who had come from northern and western Europe, but that after 1890 a greater proportion of immigrants were coming from southern and eastern European countries and from parts of Asia. These immigrants generally held religious beliefs which were not Protestant and political values which may have been different from those subscribed to by most Americans. The impact of the Emergency Quota Act of 1921 and the Johnson–Reed Act of 1924 was to massively reduce the total number of all immigrants entering the country, but to disproportionately cut the numbers entering from southern and eastern Europe and Asia.

Crime and Prohibition

From its introduction in 1919 (see page 18) to its repeal in 1933 (see page 54) Prohibition was consistently undermined throughout the 1920s. This was due to a number of factors.

Law breaking and problems of enforcement

The production and selling of alcohol were deemed to be crimes under Prohibition legislation but drinking alcohol was not a crime which meant that many were prepared to carry on drinking. Certain immigrant groups in working-class areas continued to drink, while middle-class people went to '**speakeasies**' such as the Cotton Club. Penalties for breaking the law were not harsh either. Police and judges were bribed and there were only 1500 federal agents employed to enforce Prohibition. Bill McCoy, a rum runner in the Bahamas, had faster boats than the agents, and the sheer scope of the USA's landed borders plus 29,000 km of coastline made it incredibly difficult for federal agents to enforce Prohibition. The Purple Gang, for example, ran alcohol across the Detroit River from Canadian distilleries.

The cost of enforcement went from $4.4 million to $13.4 million during the 1920s, but this was still not enough to deal with lawbreakers.

Growth of organised crime

Organised crime grew up around large **bootlegging** operations. For example, the Torrio–Capone gang of Chicago was the first big criminal organisation to capitalise on Prohibition. Gang violence reached its peak with the St Valentine's Day massacre in 1929 when members of Capone's gang killed six members of the rival North Side 'Bugs' Moran gang. Capone's criminal activities were not of course confined to alcohol, and included prostitution and gambling. Prohibition had been introduced in part to reduce violent crime, but the homicide rate nearly doubled from 5.6 per 100,000 in the 1900s to 10 per 100,000 during the 1920s, and Prohibition would be forever linked to crime in the minds of the American people.

Political corruption

Corruption was endemic at all levels of politics. Capone put his gunmen on roofs on polling day in Chicago. He 'bought off' Bill Thompson, the Chicago mayor, and purchased the *Cicero Tribune* newspaper to stop its campaign against him. Members of the Ohio Gang (President Harding's ruling clique), such as Attorney General Harry Daugherty, were bribed by whisky maker George Remus.

Support for the repeal of Prohibition

Opponents of Prohibition gradually became more vociferous. The National Association Against the Prohibition Amendment was set up in 1918 and the Women's Organisation for National Prohibition Reform, founded in 1929, had 100,000 members within weeks and made repeal respectable. Rising unemployment towards the end of the 1920s made people think about the jobs alcohol manufacture could provide, as well as the taxes which might accrue should alcohol be legalised. In the 1928 presidential election Al Smith stood for the Democrats as a **wet** candidate.

Medical problems

It is estimated that unregulated poisonous 'rot gut' liquor killed more than 4000 people in 1925 compared to just over 1000 in 1920.

Alcohol consumption increased

Despite an initial drop, the consumption of alcohol increased during the 1920s. There was also a shift in drinking trends away from beer towards spirits which were relatively less bulky to transport and conceal, and these spirits were often stronger in terms of alcohol content. In New Jersey it was said that there were ten times as many places where one could get a drink than there were before Prohibition.

Prioritisation

Below are a sample exam-style 12-mark question and a list of reasons that could be used in the answer. Demonstrating prioritisation is one way of structuring the answer to an 'Explain why' question. Using your own knowledge and the information on the opposite page, decide the order of priority you would give to these factors. Write numbers on the spectrum below to indicate their relative importance and, beneath each, briefly justify that factor's placement, demonstrating why you feel some factors are more important than others.

Explain why the enforcement of Prohibition was undermined during the 1920s.

1. Organised crime and violence
2. Problems of enforcement
3. Anti-Prohibition campaign groups
4. Attitudes of politicians and corruption
5. Increase in alcohol consumption
6. Health-related problems

Most important   Least important

Identify an argument

Below are a sample exam-style 24-mark question and two sample paragraphs. One suggests a high-level answer because it advances a supported argument. The other suggests a low-level answer because it contains only description and assertion. Identify which is which. The definitions below should help you:

- **Argument**: giving a view supported by reasoning and detailed evidence
- **Assertion**: giving a view which is not supported by reasoning and evidence
- **Description**: providing facts which do not support a view.

How far did the growth of organised crime undermine the success of Prohibition in the period up to 1929?

Paragraph 1

Organised crime pre-dated Prohibition, but the opportunity to manufacture and distribute illicit alcohol turned gang leaders such as Al Capone into rich and powerful men who were able seemingly to defy the law and to undermine the Prohibition experiment in the USA. It can be argued that organised crime undermined Prohibition in two main ways: by manufacturing and selling liquor, which in itself broke the law, and by forever linking Prohibition to the growth of crime and violence in the eyes of the American people.

Paragraph 2

During the 1920s organised crime grew and became more violent. Al Capone was the leading gangster in Chicago during the 1920s and he gave orders for the St Valentine's Day massacre in 1929 when his hired killers gunned down some members of the North Side Moran gang. Capone's crime empire made money from bootlegging, prostitution and gambling.

The continuing problems in agriculture and parts of the economy

The term 'conspicuous consumption', first coined by economist Thorstein Veblen in 1899, can well be applied to the increased demand for consumer goods in the 1920s. It was, however, a lifestyle which remained alien to many millions of Americans. By 1929 it is estimated that:

- 12 million American families lived below the **poverty line**
- 5 per cent of Americans received a third of all income generated in the country
- the poorest 40 per cent of families received 12.5 per cent of the country's income
- the share of the national income that went to the poorest 60 per cent fell by 13 per cent between 1918 and 1929.

In particular farmers, some industrial workers, African Americans and Native Americans did not benefit from the boom.

Farmers

Farmers had prospered during the First World War with prices rising significantly between 1913 and 1917, but prices fell once the war had ended as other countries recovered and began to produce more themselves. The Fordney–McCumber tariff of 1922 led to other countries imposing tariffs on American agricultural products which made it more difficult for farmers to export, as did increased competition from Canada and overproduction. Prohibition damaged grain production as the demand for large supplies of grain from the distillers and brewers simply stopped. The greater use of machinery in agriculture increased production but meant that prices dropped further because there was more produce on the market.

Attempts by the government to aid farmers, such as the Agricultural Credits Act in 1923 and the Capper–Volstead Act of 1923, never did enough. In 1924 alone about 600,000 farmers lost their farms, and by 1929 the agricultural workforce had fallen by 5 per cent.

Workers in certain areas and industries

Certain industries went into decline such as coal and construction in the face of foreign competition. Very poor areas included the textile towns of New England, the Appalachian region of West Virginia and Kentucky and the rural South in general.

The Red Scare and the strikes during 1919 put people off unions, and union membership fell from 5.03 million to 3.6 million in the 1920s, which further disempowered workers. 'Yellow dog' contracts in which workers agreed not to strike were also recognised by the courts. Government tended to be anti-union and Attorney General Harry Daugherty in 1922 ended a railroad strike by using a judge to grant an injunction against it. Rural areas also seemed to be hit disproportionately by the failure of small banks, 500 of which failed on average every year during the 1920s. Unskilled **new immigrants** in big cities tended to find it hard to get work and increased mechanisation generally reduced the demand for skilled labour.

African Americans and Native Americans

Despite the large migration of African Americans to northern cities at the beginning of the twentieth century, most remained in the South as **sharecroppers** at the bottom of the economic pile. Nearly a million more African Americans would migrate north during the 1920s to such cities as Detroit, Chicago and New York, but even there they tended to get the worst paid jobs and live in the poorest parts of the cities. Native Americans were often confined to reservations which had a high incidence of alcoholism, crime and infant death.

! Turning statements into reasons

Below are a sample exam-style 12-mark question and a series of statements.
Read the question and turn each of the statements into a relevant reason that
could be used in the answer.

Explain why some Americans did not benefit from the economic boom
of the 1920s.

STATEMENT	REASON
The poorest 40% of families received 12.5% of the country's income during the 1920s.	
Farm prices fell once the war had ended.	
The Fordney–McCumber tariff of 1922 raised prices on foreign food coming into the USA.	
Prohibition was introduced in the 1920s.	
Agriculture became more mechanised.	
Unions were weak during the period.	
Lots of banks failed during the 1920s.	
Many African Americans worked as sharecroppers in the South.	

! Complete the paragraph

Below are a sample exam-style 24-mark question and the outline of a paragraph written
in answer to this question. The paragraph begins with a relevant comment in relation
to the question and ends with a further link. However, it lacks supporting examples.
Complete the paragraph by providing some factual detail in the space provided.

How far did farmers suffer more than other Americans during the 1920s?

It can certainly be argued that many Americans missed out on the
prosperity of the 1920s. African Americans, for example, remained
poor, while unskilled immigrants in big cities tended to be easily
exploited. Evidence from the period would, however, suggest that
farmers suffered more than other Americans, for example ...

_____

_____

_____

_____

_____

It would therefore appear that there were many disadvantages for
farmers during the 1920s which meant that they suffered more than most.

The return to normalcy in foreign policy

Following the experience of the First World War and the subsequent economic downturn, most of the country supported **isolationism**, though President Wilson had favoured 'collective security' and prominent political figures Theodore Roosevelt and Henry Cabot Lodge favoured an alliance with Britain. Hearst newspapers had not been in favour of the First World War alliance with Britain and led the opposition to involvement in foreign affairs. By the time President Harding (1921–1923) entered the White House in March 1921, the 117,000 Americans killed in the First World War and the disillusionment with Wilson's post-war peace-making in France (see page 16) had turned most Americans away from the affairs of the wider world. Harding seemed to speak for the people when he talked of '**normalcy**' (meaning a movement away from foreign affairs and a focus on domestic affairs such as the economy).

Relations with Europe

Harding said that what the USA needed was 'not internationality but nationality'. Nonetheless, the USA remained involved in European affairs. By 1924 the USA was sending observers and delegates to certain League of Nations conferences, and had an agent in Geneva to convey US views to the League. The American-organised Dawes Plan of 1924 provided loans to the German government so that it could pay reparations to the French and British so that they, in turn, could pay off money they had borrowed from the USA. The Young Plan of 1929 further reduced and rescheduled German reparation payments.

Relations with Asia

The USA also maintained an involvement with affairs in the Far East. During the 1920s the USA feared the spread of Soviet Communism to China or Japan, and wanted to maintain the **Open Door policy** regarding China (see page 14). This was upheld by the Nine Power Treaty of 1922 and protests were made when the Japanese carried out military action in China. Charles Hughes, the US Secretary of State up until 1925, pursued a reasonably active foreign policy which included the 1921 Washington Naval Conference where the USA, Japan and Britain agreed to abolish their shipbuilding programmes and agreed a 5:3:5 ship ratio in the name of world peace. The 1924 Johnson–Reed Act (see page 28), however, was anti-Asian and was particularly resented by the Japanese. Frank Kellogg, the Secretary of State after Hughes, gave his name to the 1928 Kellogg–Briand Pact by which 60 nations, including Japan, agreed to outlaw war, but the treaty contained no binding terms and can be regarded as hollow.

Relations with the Americas

It could be said that the Monroe Doctrine which defined a US sphere of influence in Latin America and the Caribbean remained a guiding principle, and that an isolationist foreign policy was not pursued with respect to this area. This point is demonstrated by the following examples of US intervention whenever American business interests seemed to be threatened by 'political instability':

- US domination of Cuban trade continued during the 1920s.
- The USA occupied Haiti between 1915 and 1934.
- The USA occupied the Dominican Republic from 1916 to 1924.
- In 1923 Harding recognised General Obregon's Mexican government in return for some compensation for land seized in the 1910s and certain guarantees to US businesses with interests in Mexico.
- US troops were sent to Venezuela in 1923 as a show of support for dictator General Gomez when there were rumours of a revolution to overthrow him. Gomez had been accommodating to US oil companies Gulf and Pan American.
- US forces were sent to Nicaragua to support the Diaz government in 1926.

Develop the detail

Below are a sample exam-style 12-mark question and a paragraph written in answer to this. The paragraph contains a limited amount of detail. Annotate the paragraph to add additional detail to the answer.

Explain why the foreign policy of the USA became less interventionist in European affairs during the 1920s.

One reason why the USA became less interventionist was because of the number of Americans killed during the First World War. The peace-making efforts of Woodrow Wilson had also not gone down well with the American people.

You're the examiner

Below are a sample exam-style 24-mark question and a paragraph written in answer to this question. Read the paragraph and the mark scheme provided on page 3. Decide which level you would award the paragraph. Write the level below, along with a justification for your decision.

How far did the USA pursue an isolationist foreign policy during the 1920s?

It could be said that although the USA steered away from active involvement in European affairs during the 1920s largely as a result of the experience of the First World War, and a reluctance to be involved in the post-war peace-making in Paris, the Monroe Doctrine remained a guiding principle with regards to Latin America and the Caribbean area. In other words, it cannot be argued that the US government pursued an isolationist foreign policy with regards to this part of the world. This is well exemplified by the American occupation of Haiti between 1915 and 1934, and the Dominican Republic from 1916 to 1924, and of course the US dominance of Cuban affairs during the 1920s continued. Mexico, which bordered the USA, remained of particular interest to US businesses and the Republican governments of the decade, and it can certainly be argued strongly that an isolationist policy was not maintained in relation to Mexico. In 1923, for example, a good relationship was established with Mexico when Harding recognised General Obregon's Mexican government in return for compensation for land seized in the 1910s and certain concessions to US businesses with interests in Mexico.

Level: Reason for choosing this level:

_____

_____

Exam focus

Revised

Below is a sample A-grade essay for a 24-mark question. Read the essay and the examiner's comments around it.

How important was the role played by Republican presidents in the economic boom of the 1920s?

In an introduction you should aim to give a sense of the direction your answer will follow and a grasp of wider factors in order to provide balance.

It can be argued that the policies of at least two Republican presidents, Harding and Coolidge, did contribute to the economic boom of the 1920s but their significance needs to be measured against other factors such as the raw materials that existed in the USA and the mass production techniques of American industry.

Note that you should aim to begin each paragraph with a sentence that puts forward a point or an argument to give the paragraph a sense of direction.

Warren Harding and Calvin Coolidge were committed during the 1920s to laissez-faire policies, which advocated government intervening as little as possible in the economy and allowing the market to set prices and wages, but in some respects these presidents were prepared to intervene in the economy, and these actions in many ways were just as important as their non-intervention. For example, the Federal Aid Highway Act of 1921 aimed to create a national highway system of roads and by the end of the year more than $75 million had been spent on roads by the federal government, which was absolutely crucial in relation to the expansion of car production. Republican presidents also intervened with respect to tariffs which generally aimed to make foreign goods more expensive, thereby allowing American manufacturers to compete more effectively. The Fordney–McCumber tariff of 1922, for example, made imported food more expensive. The passage of immigration Acts such as the Emergency Quotas Act of 1921 can also be seen as examples of government intervention aimed at limiting immigration to ensure that unemployment levels did not get too high.

Good economic understanding shown.

The laissez-faire policies of Republican presidents embraced a lack of regulation of the stock market and a general reluctance to prosecute monopolies, which allowed businessmen more of a free hand to build on their wartime profits and mass production techniques. Samuel Insull, for example, came to dominate electricity production through General Electric during the period. Harding and Coolidge were also happy to allow the expansion of credit. Andrew Mellon, who was Secretary of the Treasury between 1921 and 1932, also cut taxes which left people with more money in their pockets to either spend or invest.

An element of doubt/counter-argument that the economic boom was entirely down to the presidents is introduced plus good statistical data.

As well as the role played by Republican presidents it is also important to look at longer-term factors which had little to do with the economic boom of the 1920s. During the First World War the use of mass production techniques and the profits made created an infrastructure which would underpin the growth of the 1920s. US Steel's profits more than doubled during the war, and General Motors went from a yearly profit of around $7 million before the war to an annual profit of nearly $22 million after the war. The USA was left as the major creditor nation after the war which allowed it to take advantage of debtor nations in terms of trade and undoubtedly contributed to the economic boom.

The mass production techniques that were at the heart of wartime expansion had been pioneered by entrepreneur Henry Ford who had set up the first moving assembly line in 1913 in Detroit. Ford was selling a basic Model T car for $950 in 1914, but by 1929 it cost only $290. The abundance of raw materials, such as the oilfields at Spindletop in Texas and the iron ore and coal in Pennsylvania, also allowed for industrial expansion. Car production used up 75 per cent of glass produced in the USA, 96 per cent of oil, 65 per cent of its leather, 80 per cent of its rubber and 20 per cent of its steel, and it had knock-on effects in other areas too. Cars allowed for the expansion of cities and leisure time, which might be spent by families at the cinema, which in turn stimulated the movie industry. It could be argued that without car production the boom of the 1920s would never have happened, with or without Republican presidents in office, although the expansion of the road system did owe something to presidential involvement.

The 1920s also witnessed a huge increase in consumer demand. In 1929, 80 per cent of radios were bought on credit as were 60 per cent of the 26 million cars sold. Average industrial wages went up by about $5 a week during the decade which also fuelled the consumer boom and made it an important factor in the economic boom.

Republican policies during the decade clearly helped to promote economic prosperity for many Americans, but it seems fair to say that longer-term factors such as the emergence of the car industry and the impact the First World War had on mass production played a more significant part in the boom than the presidents of the period.

Starts with link to previous paragraph, and the presidents are still included at the end to give the essay a sense of continuity.

Another factor is considered here to give the essay a bit more range.

Conclusion reaches a final decision.

24/24

This is an impressive answer which shows an understanding of debate and excellent grasp of detail. The candidate has produced an analytical and balanced answer which has covered a range of relevant factors.

Exam focus

This essay is successful because it maintains a strong focus on the question throughout. There is a lot of detail on the presidents but other paragraphs are also related to the presidents where possible. Go through the essay and underline every mention of the words 'presidents' and 'Harding' and 'Coolidge'. Next look at an essay you have written and underline your use of key words. Can you improve on your own efforts in the light of what you have seen here?

The reasons for the stock market crash and the Great Depression

Revised

What was the Wall Street Crash?

The Wall Street Crash was the dramatic fall in share prices on the American stock market over a five-day period beginning on 24 October 1929. It signalled the end of the economic boom of the 1920s and marked the beginning of a decade-long crisis known as the Great Depression. The reasons why this occurred can be split into long- and short-term causes as outlined below.

Long-term causes of the Wall Street Crash

- Speculation – ordinary Americans had never bought stocks before the 1920s. However, during the First World War they were encouraged to buy government war bonds and this created an investment culture. As American industry boomed during the 1920s, the value of shares increased and many people were encouraged to buy stocks to make a quick profit.

- Republican government policies – the Republican Party adopted a *laissez-faire* approach in the belief that the market would always sort itself out and there was no need for government intervention. Therefore there was no regulation on business activities, particularly the stock market and banking activity.

- Buying stocks on credit – as the investment culture took hold people used credit in the shape of stockbroker loans. Known as **buying on margin**, the loans had to be paid back.

- Interest rates – low interest rates made borrowing much more attractive.

Short-term causes of the Wall Street Crash

- **Tariffs** – in his election campaign of 1928 Herbert Hoover promised to increase import tariffs to help protect American business from foreign competition. When he won the election, stock market speculation about the tariff changes pushed up share prices. However, many people were opposed to the increased tariffs and on 21 October the Senate announced plans to prevent Hoover's changes. When people realised the increased tariff would not happen selling began and prices began to fall.

- Loss of confidence – by the autumn of 1929, more experienced investors began selling their stocks as they felt a crisis was looming. This caused a dip in confidence in the market which led to a downturn in investment in stocks in the weeks prior to the crash in October.

- Panic selling – on 24 October more than 12 million shares were sold triggering a selling frenzy that saw the price of shares plummet. As the stockbrokers called in the loans, referred to as a '**margin call**', this increased the panic as people tried to sell their shares in order to meet their debts before they fell even further in price. Bankers attempted to stabilise the situation by investing large sums in key businesses but this was only a temporary solution. The collapse was complete by 29 October (Black Tuesday) as 16 million shares were sold at a fraction of their purchase price.

Consequences of the crash

The crash was part of the long-term problems in the economy that created the 1920s boom. In fact between December 1929 and March 1930 the stock market had recovered around three-quarters of what it had lost in terms of share values and many believed that this was the market stabilising itself following almost a decade of unregulated speculation.

The principal consequence of the crash was to destroy confidence in both the stock market and the US economy as a whole. The big businessmen and bankers who were seen as the champions of the economic boom were now blamed for the economic problems that followed. People lost all confidence in banks and other financial institutions, taking their money out of the banks for fear of losing what little they had.

Prioritisation

Below are a sample exam-style 12-mark question and a list of reasons that could be used in the answer. Demonstrating prioritisation is one way of structuring the answer to an 'Explain why' question. Using your own knowledge and the information on the opposite page, decide the order of priority you would give to these factors. Write numbers on the spectrum below to indicate their relative importance and, beneath each, briefly justify that factor's placement, demonstrating why you feel some factors are more important than others.

Explain why the stock market crashed in 1929.

1. Increased speculation on the stock market fuelled by credit – buying on margin
2. Republican government policies and lack of regulation
3. Low interest rates that made borrowing more attractive
4. Tariffs promised by Hoover and the impact this had on investment
5. Loss of confidence just prior to the crash that led to selling stock in the weeks before October
6. Panic selling that drove share prices down further between 24 and 29 October

Most important   Least important

Identify an argument

Below is a sample exam-style 24-mark question and two sample paragraphs. One suggests a high-level answer because it advances a supported argument. The other suggests a low-level answer because it contains only description. Identify which is which. The definitions below should help:

- **Argument**: giving a view supported by reasoning and fact
- **Assertion**: giving a view that is not supported by reasoning and fact
- **Description**: providing facts but not in support of a view.

How far was the availability of easy credit the main cause of the Wall Street Crash in October 1929?

Paragraph 1

In October 1929 the economic boom of the 1920s came to an abrupt end with the Wall Street Crash. Shares were being sold in huge numbers and their value plummeted, triggering a selling frenzy that was almost certain to bring about a general collapse of the stock market. This was made much worse when the stockbrokers, who had provided the loans for people to buy shares, now insisted on these loans being paid back and the only way this could be achieved was by selling the stock that had been purchased, usually at a great loss. This only increased the panic as people tried to salvage as much as they could by selling their shares too. On 29 October, known as 'Black Tuesday', the collapse was complete as more than 16 million shares were sold.

Paragraph 2

The availability of easy credit encouraged people to buy consumer goods in increasing numbers. This discouraged saving as people no longer had to wait to buy the luxury items they desired. The availability of credit spread to the stock market and ordinary people began speculating. The system of 'buying on margin' meant that the investor need only put down a fraction of the cost of the stock with the rest being given in the form of a loan by the broker. This was risky as, if share prices dropped, as they did in October 1929, then the broker could issue a 'margin call' which meant the investor had to pay the loan back immediately and the only way to do that would be to sell their stock. Such practices were made possible by the lack of government intervention and regulation of financial institutions as the government preferred to let the market regulate itself.

The onset of the Great Depression

The Great Depression was a severe economic slump that hit America, Europe and most of the industrialised nations around the world. Beginning with the Wall Street Crash in 1929, the depression lasted ten years and was only ended by the outbreak of the Second World War.

Underlying causes

■ Farming – the American agricultural sector had reached its peak by 1920 fuelled by wartime production. From this point the sector suffered a long-term decline due to overproduction leading to a fall in grain prices. Prohibition, beginning in 1920, also hit farmers as they lost grain sales to brewers and distillers. The value of farmland also fell by 30 per cent in the decade before the Wall Street Crash leading to a shortfall between what the farmer had as a mortgage against the farm and its resalable value. Average income for farm workers was around $275 per year against a national average of $750. Farm workers therefore had little or no disposable income. Many farmers could not pay their mortgages and had to sell their farms.

■ Problems in staple industries – coalmining, shipbuilding, railroads and textiles were also either stagnating or in decline. Mechanisation increased unemployment in these sectors and wages were kept low as employers tried to maximise profits. The 1920s boom had only benefited the consumer industries and not the older staple industries. Because of their low level of income, both farm workers and those in the staple industries could not purchase the consumer goods that drove the economy in the 1920s.

■ Easy credit – as the economic boom got underway consumer goods became much more attainable as credit was widely available. A small deposit secured the goods and they could then be paid for on a weekly or monthly basis on what was called an instalment plan. This stimulated production to meet the growing demand. However, it also discouraged saving as a buy-now-pay-later mentality developed. When the stock market crashed and workers were laid off it became difficult for these people to meet their debts and many of the goods were repossessed.

Short-term causes

■ Overproduction – by the end of 1928 those people who could afford the larger consumer items such as cars, fridges and washing machines already had them. However, the rate of production continued into 1929 as production levels maintained employment. The drop in demand created a large surplus of goods and so production was scaled down in the last two months before the crash in October 1929. This led to workers being laid off which meant demand for goods fell even further.

■ The Wall Street Crash – considered to be the beginning of the Great Depression, the crash was a psychological blow to the American economy. (See section on the Wall Street Crash, page 38.)

■ Banking crisis – many ordinary banks had used their customers' money to invest in the stock market in order to increase profits. When the stock market crashed this left the banks in crisis as they had insufficient funds with which to repay their customers. As word spread there began a run on the banks as people rushed to withdraw their savings before the bank collapsed. Ironically, it was this action that increased the likelihood of a banking collapse with thousands of banks closing during 1930–1931. Approximately 10 million individual savings accounts were lost and many businesses also collapsed as they could no longer obtain loans and establish a line of credit.

Long-term or short-term?

Below is a sample exam-style 12-mark question, which asks for a range of reasons. Understanding the difference between long-term and short-term factors helps give structure to an answer to an 'Explain why' question. The chart that follows offers a list of reasons that are relevant to the answer to the question. Using the information on the opposite page and your own knowledge, decide whether each reason should be considered a long- or short-term factor and tick the appropriate box.

Explain why the Great Depression hit America.

	LONG-TERM	SHORT-TERM
1. Problems in agriculture (farming)		
2. Banking crisis		
3. The Wall Street Crash		✓
4. Easy credit		
5. Problems in the staple industries		
6. Overproduction		

Turning assertion into argument

Below are a sample exam-style 24-mark question and a series of assertions. Read the question and then add a justification to turn it into a supported view, so creating an argument.

How far was the onset of the Great Depression caused by underlying factors?

The Great Depression was caused by the stagnation of staple industries ...

_____

_____

As the economic boom got underway consumer goods became more widely available due to easy credit ...

_____

_____

However, overproduction by the end of the 1920s was also a major problem ...

_____

_____

Impact of the Great Depression

Revised

The Great Depression had an enormous impact on various aspects of American society and government policy throughout the 1930s. America's GDP, a measure used to determine a country's income and economic growth, dropped from $104 billion in 1929 to $56 billion by 1932.

Workers

Around 25 per cent of America's working population became unemployed at the height of the depression in 1933. Many of these workers became displaced and separated from their families as they roamed America looking for work. Makeshift shantytowns, which became known as 'Hoovervilles', began to spring up as the homeless made homes out of cardboard and other discarded materials they could find.

Farmers

Farmers never enjoyed the economic boom of the 1920s. Their plight deepened as a result of the depression. Farmers in the Midwest were hit by a series of droughts beginning in 1930. This dried up the soil and created the conditions for the **Dust Bowl** that hit the region in 1935. Congress passed the Hawley–Smoot Tariff which pushed import duties to extremely high levels. This made the situation worse for farmers as they could not export grain as other countries put up tariffs of their own in response which decreased export sales. Many farmers in the Midwest left their farms as they could no longer make a living or pay their mortgages. On the other hand, farmers in the Tennessee Valley region suffered from flooding which destroyed crops and washed away acres of topsoil.

Foreign policy

The depression caused the USA to retreat further into **isolationism** which affected its foreign policy, as it took no major action in response to the international crises of the 1930s, such as the Japanese invasion of Manchuria in 1931, Italian invasion of Abyssinia in 1935 and the growth and expansion of Nazi Germany. The USA also passed a series of Neutrality Acts to distance itself from potential conflicts (see Page 60). The misery of the depression would last until the outbreak of the Second World War.

Mind map

Below are a sample exam-style 12-mark question and the beginnings of a mind map to identify relevant reasons. Read the question and complete the mind map with a sentence of explanation. Then prioritise your reasons by adding numbers to each oval – with 1 as the most important reason and 6 as the least important.

Explain why the Great Depression had such a huge impact on American society.

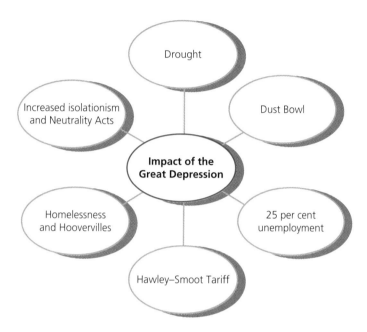

Turning assertion into argument   **a**

Below are a sample exam-style 24-mark question and a series of assertions. Read the question and then add a justification to each of the assertions to turn it into a supported view, so creating an argument.

How far were farmers the worst hit by the Great Depression in the 1930s?

The farming sector in America never really benefited from the economic boom of the 1920s ...

_____

_____

In addition, farmers suffered a series of environmental disasters in the 1930s ...

_____

_____

However, industrial workers also suffered as the Great Depression took hold ...

_____

_____

Responses to the depression under President Hoover

Hoover's election

Calvin Coolidge decided not to run for a second term as president in 1928 and so the Republican Party chose Herbert Hoover as their candidate. This proved a popular choice and he secured the presidency with a landslide victory over his Democratic rival Al Smith, gaining 444 electoral college votes to Smith's 87. It was believed that he would continue the prosperity that America had enjoyed throughout the 1920s.

However, after just eight months in office the stock market crash signalled the beginning of the worst economic disaster in American history. Hoover initially believed that the stock market crash would be short-lived and would clean up the bad practices as the market righted itself. He believed that the American spirit of **rugged individualism** would set the country back on track.

Hoover's response during his presidency

Some historians take the view that Hoover was a 'do nothing' president who cared little for the plight of ordinary Americans. This is supported by his unwillingness, until 1932, to give direct aid to the unemployed and his treatment of the **Bonus Marchers** the same year. Others see Hoover as being much more proactive, pointing to the policies he introduced to try to ease the effects of the depression and stating that he laid the foundations for the New Deal. His key actions are outlined below:

- The Federal Farm Board (1930) provided loans to farmers and helped support and stabilise prices. However, because America, Canada and Argentina were all producing surplus grain, prices continued to fall.
- The Hawley–Smoot Tariff Act (June 1930) levied duties on imported goods. Aimed at protecting American businesses from foreign competition, it caused other countries to put up protective tariffs in response, thereby hampering American exports.
- Reliance on **voluntarism** – Hoover did not want to give direct aid to those affected by the depression in the form of unemployment payments as he believed this would create a climate of dependency. He believed that all aspects of society, businesses, charities, state and local governments should help instead.
- Income tax cuts (1930) were aimed at giving workers more disposable income to spend on consumer goods, stimulating economic growth. However, rising unemployment meant that many did not have any money to begin with and those who did tended to hoard it.
- A Public Works Program (June 1930) was initiated that included the Boulder Dam project, later renamed the Hoover Dam. It made available $900 million for this and other projects to try to provide employment.
- The Reconstruction and Finance Corporation (January 1932) was created to provide aid to railroads, businesses and financial institutions to stabilise industry. This proved unsuccessful and by the end of 1932, 25 per cent of the working-age population was unemployed.
- Tax increases on businesses, corporations and farms (July 1932) were meant to help balance the federal budget, but made things much more difficult for industry and farmers.

Response to Hoover's policies

Hoover's lack of economic aid to those unemployed and his reluctance to explain his actions caused many to resent him. His unpopularity was made worse by his treatment of the **Bonus Army** in the summer of 1932. First World War veterans who were hardest hit by the depression marched on Washington, D.C. to demand the early payment of a bonus that was due to be given in 1945. Hoover ordered the army to remove them and they used tear gas and burnt the camp to the ground. These factors helped bring defeat in the election in November 1932 as Franklin D. Roosevelt, with his promise of a 'new deal' for the American people, looked more appealing.

Mind map

Below are a sample exam-style 12-mark question and the beginnings of a mind map to identify relevant reasons. Read the question and complete the mind map with a sentence of explanation. Then prioritise your reasons by adding numbers to each oval – with 1 as the most important reason and 6 as the least important.

Explain why President Hoover was so unpopular in 1932.

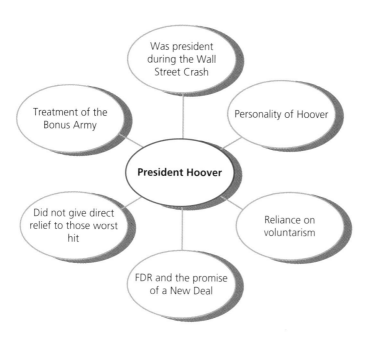

Develop the detail (a)

Below are a sample exam-style 24-mark question and a paragraph written in answer to this. The paragraph contains a limited amount of detail. Annotate the paragraph to add additional detail to the answer.

How far was Hoover's treatment of the Bonus Army the main cause of Hoover's defeat in the 1932 election?

Hoover's treatment of the Bonus Marchers in the summer of 1932, so close to the election, undoubtedly had an impact on his electoral chances, but this was more the final straw than the main cause of public discontent. His staunch belief in rugged individualism, coupled with his view that supporting businesses through the Reconstruction and Finance Corporation would in turn revive the economy, was seen as a huge failure. His decision to support higher tariffs caused further damage to the failing economy too.

Roosevelt and the New Deal

The New Deal was the major domestic policy to tackle the ravages of the Great Depression and had two phases. The First New Deal covered the period 1933 to 1934 and the Second New Deal covered the period 1935 to 1938.

Aims and objectives

The New Deal had three broad aims, often referred to as the three Rs: Relief, to give immediate aid to those worst hit; Recovery, to get the struggling economy back on its feet; Reform, to change the financial systems and introduce regulations. These were carried out by a variety of agencies which became known as the '**Alphabet Agencies**' shown in the table below.

Relief and recovery	
Act or agency	**Purpose**
Agricultural Adjustment Administration (AAA) 1933	Farmers were given subsidies to cut back production of crops, meat and dairy products. This aimed at increasing prices of farm produce by reducing overproduction. However, many African American farmers did not benefit from the same relief as white farmers, particularly in southern states.
Civilian Conservation Corps (CCC) 1933	Provided employment for young unmarried men aged 18–25 in conservation work, such as creating parks and planting trees. More than 2 million young men were employed between 1933 and 1941. However, it did not employ women and the pay was low ($30 per month).
Federal Emergency Relief Administration (FERA) 1933	Provided $500 million in federal funds to state agencies to make relief payments to the unemployed.
National Industrial Recovery Act (NIRA) June 1933	Created public works programmes such as the Public Works Administration (PWA) to help with unemployment.
Public Works Administration (PWA) 1933	Large-scale public works programme to create employment on building projects such as roads, bridges and housing. More than $4 billion had been spent by 1934 when the programme ended, although the projects continued throughout the 1930s.
Tennessee Valley Authority (TVA) 1934	Large-scale federal programme that spanned seven states through which the Tennessee River flowed. Built several dams to provide cheap hydro-electric power, prevent flooding and provide irrigation to farmlands and create employment.
Federal Housing Administration (FHA) 1934	Designed to regulate mortgages and housing conditions in order to alleviate the housing crisis caused by banks calling in mortgages, making many homeless.
Resettlement Administration (RA) May 1935	Aimed to resettle up to 450,000 farmers and their families away from the worst affected areas of the 'Dust Bowl' (see page 42). Due to the cost of the programme and reluctance of farmers to move only 5000 were resettled.
Works Progress Administration (WPA) April 1935	The largest of the public works schemes to replace the PWA. It employed 8 million unskilled men in building roads, public buildings and parks, hospitals and schools. Also helped employ writers, musicians and artists in drama and literary projects.
Social Security Act (SSA) 1935	This created a federal retirement pension system for most workers and was funded by doubling income tax on workers' wages. It also created an unemployment insurance plan to help provide temporary help to those out of work.
Reform and regulation	
Act or agency	
National Industrial Recovery Act (NIRA) June 1933	Provided regulation of industry but was declared unconstitutional by the Supreme Court in 1935 and is considered a policy failure by historians.
National Recovery Administration (NRA) June 1933	• Aimed to provide codes of practice for industry by ensuring fair competition and rates of pay, and gave workers the right to collective bargaining, in terms of wages and working conditions, through trades unions. • Established working hours and child labour under 16 was made illegal.
Banking Act (Glass–Steagall Act) June 1933	• Separated investment and commercial banking activities. Only specified investment banks were permitted to speculate on the stock market. • Provided deposit insurance for customers of up to $5000 under the Federal Deposit Insurance Corporation (FDIC).

Turning statements into reasons

Below are a sample exam-style 12-mark question and a series of statements. Read the question and turn each statement into a relevant reason so that it could be used in the answer.

Explain why some Alphabet Agencies were considered successful.

STATEMENT	REASON
The Public Works Administration (PWA) was created in 1933.	
The Works Progress Administration (WPA) had widespread appeal.	
The Tennessee Valley Authority (TVA) was successful.	
The Civilian Conservation Corps (CCC) helped young men.	

You're the examiner

Below are a sample exam-style 24-mark question and a paragraph written in answer to this question. Read the paragraph and the mark scheme provided on page 3. Using the information on the opposite page and the rest of this section, decide which level you would award the paragraph. Write the level below, along with justification for your decision.

How important were Roosevelt's New Deal policies in reducing unemployment between 1933 and 1939?

Roosevelt attempted to tackle the issue of unemployment as soon as he took office. Job creation schemes during the First New Deal through Alphabet Agencies such as the Civilian Conservation Corps (CCC) and the Public Works Administration helped millions of unemployed find work. The Tennessee Valley Authority (TVA) helped create employment in seven states in the region and protected farmland from flooding. In addition, the Farm Credit Administration helped farmers with loans to help keep them employed. The Works Progress Administration (WPA) of the Second New Deal employed some 8 million workers in a range of building programmes and this extended to artists, writers and musicians. However, there were restrictions on some agencies. The CCC only employed men aged between 18 and 25 and the rate of pay was low. In farming, white farmers benefited more from the New Deal than African American farmers. The AAA encouraged farmers to cut back production and this meant they had to lay off farm labourers as there was not as much work. While the New Deal did not get rid of unemployment between 1933 and 1939, it did relieve it somewhat and it gave the American people some hope for the future.

Level: Reason for choosing this level:

_____

_____

Successes and failures of the New Deal

Successes of the First New Deal

- It stabilised the banking sector and the system of credit during Roosevelt's first 100 days.
- It gave protection to farmers and home owners by helping them to refinance their loans and make repayments much easier.
- Public works schemes provided employment.
- Public works schemes benefited conservation (CCC) and helped with America's infrastructure through the construction of roads, hospitals and schools.
- It had a positive psychological impact on American citizens, changing the general mood from that of helplessness to optimism.

Failures of the First New Deal

- The AAA did not achieve all its aims as it was the onset of drought conditions and not federal policies that cut wheat production, making the situation of the farmers worse.
- It did little for African American farmers in the South as the land used for growing cotton was reduced and there was little direct aid as Roosevelt did not want to upset southern politicians and businessmen who may have obstructed New Deal policies.
- While it lessened the impact of the depression on people's lives it did not bring recovery in either industry or agriculture and there were 22 million people unemployed by the end of 1934.

Successes of the Second New Deal

- Government intervention helped improve labour rights and union membership increased twofold between 1935 and 1940.
- There were lasting improvements in rural electrification as 30 per cent more farms had electricity in the period between 1930 and 1945.

Failures of the Second New Deal

- Economic recovery was marginal and in fact declined between 1937 and 1939 as a second recession kicked in and unemployment rose again.
- Production levels remained below those of 1929 and did not reach the same level until 1942 as the Second World War helped increase armaments production on a massive scale.
- Farmers continued to suffer and the Resettlement Administration did little to help their plight.

How important?

Below is a sample exam-style 24-mark question which asks you about the importance of a factor. Questions like this can be answered by balancing the way the factor was important against the ways in which it was not. A series of statements relevant to the question are given below. Using your own knowledge and the information on the previous pages, decide whether these statements suggest a factor was important or not important and tick the appropriate box.

How important were public works programmes under the New Deal in reducing unemployment in the USA in the years 1933 to 1941?

	IMPORTANT	NOT IMPORTANT
1. TVA provided employment in the Tennessee Valley area, covering several states.		
2. Farmers were given help/loans to keep their farms going and maintain employment.		
3. CCC was limited to a specific age range.		
4. The WPA, set up in 1935, provided employment for a range of people.		
5. Various job creation schemes were set up during the period to ease unemployment (PWA, CCC, TVA and WPA).		

 Identify an argument (a)

Below is a sample exam-style 24-mark question and two sample paragraphs. One suggests a high-level answer because it advances a supported argument. The other suggests a low-level answer because it contains description and assertion. Identify which is which. The definitions below should help you:

● **Argument**: giving a view supported by reasoning and fact

● **Assertion**: giving a view that is not supported by reasoning and fact

● **Description**: providing facts but not in support of a view.

How successful were the policies of President Franklin D. Roosevelt in bringing about economic recovery in the years 1933 to 1941?

Paragraph 1

Roosevelt began straight away by attempting to stabilise the financial system and stop banks from collapsing. He also tried to get people back to work with various public works schemes across America. He gave help to farmers and homeowners by helping them meet mortgage repayments to stop them being repossessed. However, not all the public works schemes worked and unemployment went up between 1937 and 1939. It was only after 1939 that the economy really started to improve.

Paragraph 2

The first thing Roosevelt did during his first 100 days was to stabilise the banking system through the passage of the Emergency Banking Act which initiated a national banking holiday which closed down all the nation's banks for four days to prevent them from collapsing. Only those with sufficient funds were allowed to reopen after that period. He also initiated public works schemes such as the PWA, the CCC, the TVA and the WPA to get people back to work and give them hope. In general terms, this dramatically reduced unemployment, with the exception of a slight increase between 1937 and 1939, as a second-wave recession hit America. However, Roosevelt did not solve the economic problems and production levels remained below those of 1929, only reaching them in 1942. It took an outside event in the form of the Second World War and the need for large-scale rearmament to truly end the depression.

Opposition to the policies of the New Deal from the left

Opposition to the New Deal programme came from:

- the left of Roosevelt's own Democratic Party
- socialists
- communists
- the right-wing conservative Republicans
- the Supreme Court
- big business
- the **Liberty League**.

Those on the left accused Roosevelt of not going far enough with his relief programmes and those on the right accused him of going too far and creating a nation dependent on government handouts. Roosevelt also faced opposition from a conservative dominated Supreme Court who struck down a number of his policies during the First New Deal in particular.

Impact of opposition from the left

While pressure from these groups and individuals no doubt helped push Roosevelt into pursuing more radical legislation after 1934, such as the Social Security Act, the political challenge to him was minimal, at least following the assassination of Huey Long.

- Socialists and communists wanted an end to the **capitalist economic system** that they felt was corrupt and damaged beyond repair following the stock market crash and the onset of the depression. They looked towards the Soviet Union as an example of good economic planning as it appeared unaffected by the market forces of capitalism that had brought American and western economic systems to their knees. In reality they had very little impact on the New Deal policies due to lack of popular support and a general fear and suspicion of communism.

- Dr Francis Townsend, a retired Californian doctor, put forward a plan that he believed would stimulate the economy and increase domestic demand. He proposed that all those over the age of 60 should receive a monthly pension of $200 provided they spent the money within 30 days. Not surprisingly more than half a million old people supported Townsend and a bill was proposed in the House of Representatives based on his plan. Although it was not passed, a scaled-down version of his plan was adopted through the Social Security Act of 1935.

- Father Charles Coughlin was initially a supporter of the New Deal, but became critical of Roosevelt through his weekly radio programme which attracted 35 million listeners. He accused Roosevelt of being influenced by the major bankers who he blamed for the depression. He called for the **nationalisation** of industry, inflationary measures to be implemented and greater use of silver coinage. He became more **anti-Semitic** in his views of the administration, criticising Henry Morgenthau, the Secretary of the Treasury, and made comments favourable to the fascist governments of Hitler and Mussolini. As America entered the war, his broadcasts were brought to an end by the National Association of Broadcasters and he was told by the Catholic Church to cease his political activities or face being '**defrocked**'.

- Senator Huey P. Long, a critic from within Roosevelt's own party, launched the 'Share Our Wealth' campaign in 1934 which promoted a $5000 homestead allowance and a minimum wage of $2500 per year to all workers. It would be financed by increasing income and inheritance taxes on the wealthy of 1 per cent over $1 million, increasing by 1 per cent for each million to a maximum of $8 million. Anything over that amount would be taxed at 100 per cent. The plan could have cost Roosevelt the support of some sections of big business. Long's plan had significant support among the working classes and he was considered a serious challenger to Roosevelt for the 1936 election. However, he was assassinated in September 1935 by Carl Weiss, the son-in-law of one of Long's opponents, Judge Benjamin Pavy, whom Long had threatened.

Creating a Venn diagram **a**

Below is a sample exam-style 12-mark question. Use your own knowledge and the information on the opposite page to produce a Venn diagram plan for an answer to this question which groups the reasons thematically.

Explain why there was opposition to the New Deal from the left between 1933 and 1941.

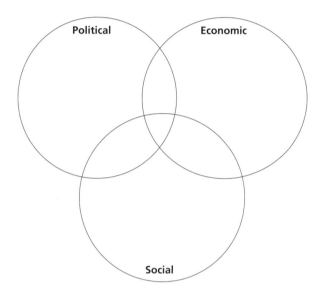

 Make the links **a**

Below are a sample exam-style 12-mark question and a series of relevant reasons that could be used in the answer. Read the question and add a comment and linking phrase to each reason and show how it relates to the following one.

Explain why some influential individuals were critical of the New Deal.

Reason	Comment and linking phrase leading to the next reason
Dr Francis Townsend was concerned with the impact the depression was having on the elderly and felt the New Deal was not doing enough to address this.	
Father Charles Coughlin felt that Roosevelt was being influenced by the bankers in producing his New Deal policies.	
Huey Long was a major critic of the New Deal and felt it did not go far enough in helping the working class.	

Opposition to the policies of the New Deal from the right and Supreme Court

Revised

Impact of opposition from the right

While individual states could delay implementation of New Deal policies or interpret them differently, the Republican Party and business interests were never in a position to cause Roosevelt many problems during the 1930s.

- The Republican Party opposed many of Roosevelt's policies during the 1930s, believing government intervention had gone too far, was un-American and socialist in nature. However, the 1936 elections had brought Democratic dominance to both houses of Congress and the Republican presidential challenger, Alfred Langdon, was a poor political opponent, making the Republicans largely ineffective.

- Roosevelt faced opposition from state legislatures, particularly those in the South. When the New Deal provided some public assistance to black southerners and when Roosevelt's wife, Eleanor, spoke out against racial discrimination, white southerners believed the New Deal was a threat to states' rights and their supremacy in the South.

- When New Deal policies allowed greater union organisation and the right to collective bargaining, business leaders were outraged. They were also opposed to greater control over trade.

Big business did challenge Roosevelt's policies through the courts, often with success, which caused him to refine his policies.

- The Liberty League was perhaps the most notable opponent on the right. It was made up mostly of Republican politicians and industrialists but it also included members of Roosevelt's own Democratic Party such as Al Smith. The main aim of the League was to uphold the Constitution against New Deal policies that might undermine it and give too much power to the president. Its aim was to challenge FDR in the 1936 presidential election and when it failed, by a large margin, it began to collapse.

Impact of opposition from the Supreme Court

Many of Roosevelt's New Deal policies enacted between 1933 and 1937 were successfully challenged in the Supreme Court. In 1937 Roosevelt attempted to stop this by appointing Supreme Court Justices who were favourable towards him in his **court packing scheme**. This failed and damaged his reputation in Congress. The general impact of the Supreme Court was that during the Second New Deal, legislation was drafted much more carefully in order to avoid being declared unconstitutional and being struck down.

New Deal Act or agency	Supreme Court decision
National Industrial Recovery Act (NIRA)	*Schechter Poultry Corporation v. United States*, May 1935 Schechter Poultry, based in Brooklyn, New York, was alleged to have sold chickens unfit for consumption to a local butcher. Schechter Poultry Co. was charged by the federal government which argued that under the NIRA, Schechter Poultry can be regulated by the federal government. As Schechter only conducted trade in New York State, the Supreme Court ruled the NIRA unconstitutional as the federal government, according to the Constitution, could not regulate trade within a state (intrastate); it could only regulate trade between states (interstate). The Act was therefore invalid. This had the support of big business leaders.
Agricultural Adjustment Administration (AAA)	*United States v. Butler*, January 1936 The AAA provided payments to farmers to stop producing certain crops. Payments were financed from taxes imposed on processors and these taxes were imposed directly on farmers. Butler, a processor, refused to pay the tax and the federal government took him to court. In his defence Butler claimed that tax may not be used to transfer wealth directly from one person to another. The Supreme Court agreed with Butler and struck down the Agricultural Adjustment Act of 1933 as unconstitutional.

However, from 1937 there was a change in the attitude of the Supreme Court. It upheld a minimum wage Act passed by the state of Washington and, to the surprise of many Americans, it upheld the Wagner Act of 1935. The Wagner Act established the National Labor Relations Board (NLRB) to protect the rights of workers to organise, bargain collectively and strike. As a result, the Second New Deal did not suffer the same fate as the first at the hands of the Supreme Court.

Make the links

Below is a sample exam-style 12-mark question and a series of relevant reasons that could be used in the answer. Read the question and add a comment and linking phrase to each reason to explain it and show how it relates to the following one.

Explain why there was opposition to the New Deal from the right between 1933 and 1941.

Reason	Comment and linking phrase leading to the next reason
The Republican Party was opposed to New Deal policies.	
Big business resented government intervention.	
Some states feared that the New Deal threatened their rights under the Constitution.	
The Liberty League wanted to curb growing presidential power.	

 Complete the paragraph

Below is a sample exam-style 24-mark question and the outline of a paragraph written in answer to this question. The paragraph begins with a relevant comment in relation to the question and ends with a further link. However, it lacks supporting examples. Complete the paragraph by providing some factual detail in the space provided.

How far did the Supreme Court affect Roosevelt's New Deal policies between 1933 and 1938?

A number of Roosevelt's New Deal policies were successfully challenged in the Supreme Court and affected federal control of trade, working conditions and taxation which the federal government thought it had established with the passage of legislation through Congress.

_____

_____

_____

However, many of his New Deal policies were rebranded, such as the Agricultural Administration Act of 1938, and Supreme Court opposition was less pronounced between 1936 and the outbreak of the Second World War.

The reasons for the end of Prohibition

In December 1933 the Eighteenth Amendment was repealed by the Twenty-first Amendment and Prohibition came to an end. The factors that led to its repeal are outlined below.

Shift in public opinion

It became clear by the end of the 1920s that many of the reasons put forward for Prohibition, such as increased productivity, better health and a reduction in crime, had not materialised. The '**noble experiment**' was now widely seen as a failure, particularly as organised crime flourished under the ban. The St Valentine's Day Massacre in 1929 (see page 30) highlighted the control organised crime had over the illegal alcohol trade.

The enforcement of the law was based on class distinctions – the rich could have a well-stocked wine cellar and were unlikely to face problems. This helped shape public opinion that the **Volstead Act**, which enforced the Eighteenth Amendment, was unevenly applied, targeted the working classes and helped develop corruption at all levels of society.

Pressure groups and the growth of repeal organisations

As Prohibition did not eradicate social issues such as crime, poor health and drunkenness, groups began to organise for its repeal. Some of these groups were controlled by women, such as the Women's Committee for Repeal of the Eighteenth Amendment and the Women's Organization for National Prohibition Reform (WONPR). Widespread disregard for the law, corruption and underground drinking was not the ideal that most of the prohibitionists had campaigned for and by 1933 the WONPR, led by Pauline Sabin, had more than 1.5 million members. Women were much more powerful having gained the vote following the Nineteenth Amendment (1920), and so politicians had to take notice. The American Federation of Labor, one of the first unions in America, set up a National Committee for the Modification of the Volstead Act arguing that it restricted individual rights given by the Constitution. Other groups added to the growing call for repeal, such as:

■ the Crusaders
■ the Association Against the Prohibition Amendment (AAPA)
■ the Republican Citizens Committee Against National Prohibition.

Business elites

Some of the big industrialists who had supported Prohibition now had a change of heart. J.D. Rockefeller Jr had donated more than $500,000 to the Anti-Saloon League in its fight for national Prohibition. He now called for its repeal in a letter to a friend that was published in the *New York Times* in 1932 stating his disappointment in the growth of **speakeasies**, increased crime and a general disregard for the law as a result of Prohibition. Pierre du Pont of General Motors also campaigned for repeal at the head of the Association Against the Prohibition Amendment (AAPA) and it has been argued by historians that this was one of the most influential groups at the time.

Economic considerations

The loss of state and federal revenue was huge during the era of Prohibition. For example, New York had received almost 75 per cent of its revenue from tax on alcohol sales and Prohibition had cost the federal government $11 billion in lost taxation. In addition it cost more than $300 million to enforce. Economic issues took on greater importance as the Great Depression took hold of America.

Political factors

The hypocrisy of Congressional members came to light in 1930 in a series of newspaper articles that appeared in the *Washington Post* entitled 'The Man in the Green Hat'. The man, George Cassiday, had been supplying senators and congressmen, the very people making Prohibition laws, with illegal alcohol for ten years. This was a contributing factor to the Republican defeat in the mid-term elections and their replacement by '**wet**' Democrat candidates.

Prioritisation

Below are a sample exam-style 12-mark question and a list of reasons that could be used in the answer. Demonstrating prioritisation is one way of structuring the answer to an 'Explain why' question. Using your own knowledge and the information on the opposite page, decide the order of priority you would give to these factors. Write numbers on the spectrum below to indicate their relative importance and, beneath each, briefly justify that factor's placement, demonstrating why you feel some factors are more important than others.

Explain why Prohibition was brought to an end in December 1933.

1. Pressure groups and the growth of repeal organisations
2. Business elite

3. Huge shift in public opinion
4. Economic considerations
5. Political factors

Most important   Least important

Turning assertion into argument   (a)

Below are a sample exam-style 24-mark question and a series of assertions. Read the question and then add a justification to each of the assertions to turn it into a supported view, so creating an argument.

How important was public opinion in the repeal of Prohibition in December 1933?

By the end of the 1920s, the view of most of the general public was that Prohibition was a failure ...

_____

_____

Congress was seen as being hypocritical in making Prohibition laws ...

_____

_____

Prohibition had an economic impact on the federal government...

_____

_____

The fight against organised crime

The response of the federal government

The response of the federal government to organised crime in the 1930s was largely a reaction to the public opinion that crime was undermining society. Public perception of crime was warped by the media and films such as *Little Caesar* and *Scarface,* both made in 1931, which showed gangsters one step ahead of the law. President Hoover was determined to bring down Al Capone, which he did in 1931, and Roosevelt took up the fight in 1933, with Homer Cummings, his Attorney General, declaring a war on crime.

Organised crime and the FBI

The fight against organised crime was led by J. Edgar Hoover, who was head of the Bureau of Investigation, renamed the Federal Bureau of Investigation (FBI) in 1935. The FBI developed scientific methods to help find and convict criminals and opened a forensic laboratory in 1932. High-profile cases helped enhance the reputation of the FBI and the fight against organised crime:

- Machine Gun Kelly – gangster and armed robber arrested in 1933.
- John Dillinger – armed robber shot dead by the FBI as he left a cinema in 1934.
- Ma Barker – mother of the leaders of the **Barker-Karpis gang** shot dead by the FBI in 1935.
- Alvin Karpis – one of the leaders of the Barker-Karpis gang arrested by the FBI in 1936.

All of these cases received high-profile press coverage and numerous films were produced, under government pressure, which portrayed the FBI as successful.

Organised crime – myth and reality

Many myths existed about organised crime:

- Organised crime was confronted and defeated by individuals such as Elliott Ness and his Untouchables and the shrewdness of J. Edgar Hoover and the FBI.
- The capture or deaths of Dillinger, Kelly and Karpis were landmark events in the fight against organised crime.

However, the reality was somewhat different:

- There was no clear victory for the government in the fight against organised crime.
- Because of the repeal of Prohibition organised crime was much less visible.
- Al Capone was caught and tried for income tax evasion and the man behind this was the Inland Revenue Service (IRS) agent Frank J. Wilson, not the FBI or Ness.
- Dillinger, Kelly and Karpis were part of Prohibition-era gangs, mostly operating in the Midwest, and not part of the organised crime that the government aimed to bring down.
- Organised crime remained and was still powerful.

Why was the fight against organised crime so difficult?

A number of factors made the fight against organised crime difficult for Roosevelt during his time as president and these are outlined below:

- The amount of money available to the federal government for law enforcement, amid the grip of the Great Depression, was a fraction compared to that of organised crime.
- Bribery and corruption at the federal level among law enforcement officers, especially during the depression, meant that crime gangs were protected.
- Murder, robbery and a host of other crimes came under state law and corruption at this level meant that the federal government had no control in these areas. This was shown in the trial of Al Capone who was never convicted of murder as he had corrupted most state officials.

Below is a sample exam-style 12-mark question and a series of relevant reasons that could be used in the answer. Read the question and add a comment and linking phrase to each reason to explain it and show how it relates to the following one.

Explain why it was difficult for the federal government to deal with organised crime.

Reason	Comment and linking phrase leading to the next reason
Funding for law enforcement was poor.	
Bribery and corruption at the federal level was still a major problem.	
Most crimes were the responsibility of individual states.	

Below are a sample exam-style 24-mark question and the outline of a paragraph in answer to this question. The paragraph begins with a relevant comment in relation to the question and ends with a further link. However, it lacks supporting examples. Complete the paragraph by providing some factual detail in the space provided.

How far was the federal government successful in ending organised crime between 1931 and 1941?

The fight against organised crime between 1931 and 1941 appeared to be successful. High-profile cases, such as the trial of Al Capone in 1931 and the series of arrests or shootings of criminal gang leaders such as John Dillinger and Machine Gun Kelly, certainly appeared to prove this. However, the success the government enjoyed was limited.

_____

_____

_____

As a result, organised crime remained intact during the period 1931 to 1941 and was still a powerful force.

Exam focus

Below is a sample A-grade essay for a 24-mark question. Read the essay and the examiner's comments around it.

How successful were opponents of the New Deal in achieving their aims in the years 1933 to 1941?

Good opening paragraph that details the opposition Roosevelt faced during the period in question.

> Roosevelt faced a variety of opposition to his New Deal policies from both the right and the left of politics and also the Supreme Court. Some opposition even cut across party lines from organisations such as the Liberty League and this also included some key leaders of big business. The main aim of this opposition was to change Roosevelt's policies in line with their own views.

This paragraph details opposition from the left and assesses its impact.

> The view of the left was that Roosevelt had not gone far enough in his policies to help the poor and those affected most by the depression. Ideas put forward such as Huey Long's 'Share Our Wealth' scheme were far too radical to be considered but did have some support. However, the plan for a pension scheme by Dr Francis Townsend to give people over 60 $200 per month which they had to spend within 30 days to stimulate the economy was put forward to Congress. Although it was not taken up it was incorporated into the Social Security Act of 1935 and so this had some impact on policy making and therefore some success in influencing policy.

Here the focus is on opposition from the right and again the paragraph assesses its impact.

> The right felt that Roosevelt had intervened too much, particularly in business affairs, and some business leaders actually backed individual challenges to New Deal policies through the Supreme Court. For example, their support in Schechter Poultry Corporation v. United States in May 1935 was a successful challenge to Roosevelt's policy on trade as the NIRA, which sought to regulate trade within states, was declared unconstitutional. The Liberty League sought to challenge Roosevelt directly for the presidential election of 1936 in an attempt to bring an end to his policies. They gave their support to the Republican candidate, Alfred Langdon, but this proved unsuccessful as Roosevelt's popularity was high and he won the election with a landslide victory. The Liberty League did not mount another challenge.

The Supreme Court was perhaps the most successful opponent of the New Deal as it had the authority to declare some of Roosevelt's policies unconstitutional, such as the Agricultural Administration Agency (AAA) and the National Industrial Recovery Act (NIRA), and so forced his administration to draft policies much more carefully. However, Roosevelt was able to reintroduce the Acts thrown out by the Supreme Court in a redrafted format and he also proposed an amendment to increase the number of court justices from nine to fifteen. During the Second New Deal Roosevelt was able to push through his policies with little interference from the Supreme Court between 1937 and 1939.

The aims of the opposition to the New Deal were not fully realised as Roosevelt remained in place and so did the New Deal programme. However, it did have some impact on the policies themselves, such as the Social Security Act of 1935, and forced his administration to think much more carefully about detailed legislation. The fact that Roosevelt won the 1936 election by such a large margin suggests that he had popular support for his policies.

24/24

This is a good concise answer that shows the candidate has understood the question. The candidate has produced a balanced piece and the judgement in the conclusion reflects this. Therefore it would receive full marks.

Find the evidence

The most important element in producing an argument is providing supporting evidence and examples. Read the essay again and indentify where evidence has been used effectively to support a point.

Section 4:
The impact of the Second World War on the USA, 1941–1945

The debate concerning the end of isolationism

US isolationism in the 1920s

Isolationism was adopted as part of US foreign policy at the beginning of the 1920s. Many in the USA felt that they had been pulled into the First World War by the European powers and the bankers and financiers at home.

Nevertheless, it became evident as the 1920s wore on that the USA could not remain completely isolated in its foreign policy. The USA:

■ hosted the Naval Disarmament Conference in Washington in 1921

■ tried to secure agreement on the **Open Door policy** with regard to China

■ became involved in restructuring Germany's economy in 1924 (Dawes Plan) and in 1929 (Young Plan)

■ helped promote the Kellogg–Briand Pact in 1928.

How far was the USA isolationist in the 1930s?

As the 1930s dawned, foreign policy was not a high priority for most Americans. The Wall Street Crash and the onset of the Great Depression made domestic issues much more pressing. As fascism and militarism became dominant in Europe and the Far East, the USA watched and became determined to stay out of any future conflict. Concerned about the events in Europe, such as German rearmament, Congress passed a series of Neutrality Acts between 1935 and 1939 to make sure the USA avoided any foreign entanglements and the mistakes that brought the USA into the First World War. Those who supported continued isolation included the **America First Committee**. This had 850,000 members at its peak by mid-1940.

The First Neutrality Act, 1935

■ This prohibited the shipping of arms to nations at war, including the victims of aggression.

■ It stated that US citizens travelling on ships belonging to belligerent nations did so at their own risk.

■ The Act was to last six months.

The Second Neutrality Act, 1936

■ This added an embargo on loans and credit to belligerent nations.

■ It did not cover civil wars such as the war in Spain, 1936–1939.

■ It did not cover materials such as trucks and oil. US companies such as Texaco, Standard Oil, Ford and General Motors used this loophole to sell such items on credit to Francisco Franco, head of the Nationalists in the Spanish Civil War.

The Third Neutrality Act, 1937

■ Provision of the first two Acts was increased to cover civil wars and did not place an expiry date on the Act.

■ Passengers were forbidden to travel on ships belonging to belligerents.

■ US ships could not transport people or goods to belligerent nations.

■ A 'cash and carry' clause allowed countries to buy arms as long as they paid in cash and transported the arms in their own ships.

Following the invasion of China by Japan in 1937, President Roosevelt (FDR) did not invoke the Act as both sides did not formally declare war. British ships were used to deliver arms to the Chinese. This interpretation of the Act angered the isolationists in Congress who claimed that Roosevelt was undermining the spirit of the law.

The Fourth Neutrality Act, 1939

■ This removed the cash and carry clause, despite FDR arguing for its retention.

Following Germany's invasion of Poland in September 1939 and the declaration of war on Germany by Britain and France, Roosevelt invoked the Act but stated to Congress that the Neutrality Acts would help Germany as the aggressor by denying aid to Britain and France. His argument won over Congress and the cash and carry clause was renewed.

Prioritisation

Below are a sample exam-style 12-mark question and a list of reasons that could be used in the answer. Demonstrating prioritisation is one way of structuring the answer to an 'Explain why' question. Using your own knowledge and the information on the opposite page, decide the order of priority you would give to these factors. Write numbers in the spectrum below to indicate their importance and, beneath each, briefly justify that factor's placement, demonstrating why you feel some factors are more important than others.

Explain why Congress passed Neutrality Acts in the years 1935 to 1937.

1. Congress wanted to make sure that bankers did not give loans to countries at war

2. Congress wanted to make sure that US citizens did not travel on ships of warring nations

3. Congress did not want to get involved in hostilities with other nations

4. Congress wanted to make sure that US manufacturers did not sell arms to countries at war

5. The USA had a tradition of isolationism

6. Domestic issues were considered more important

Most important   Least important

 You're the examiner ⓐ

Below are a sample exam-style 24-mark question and a paragraph written in answer to this question. Read the paragraph and the mark scheme on page 3. Decide which level you would award the paragraph. Write the level below with a justification for your decision.

How far were the Neutrality Acts aimed at keeping the USA out of war between 1935 and 1941?

To avoid the mistakes that brought the USA into the First World War, the Neutrality Act of 1935 sought to distance itself from nations at war through a ban on arms sales and by warning US citizens not to travel on ships of warring nations. Further amendments such as a ban on loans and credit were added to the Act in 1936 and 1937. In 1939 the cash and carry clause was removed from the Act. However, following Germany's invasion of Poland in September 1939, Roosevelt successfully persuaded Congress to reintroduce the cash and carry clause to help Britain and France as he believed that Germany was the clear aggressor.

Level: Reason for choosing this level:

_____

_____

Roosevelt and the reasons for US entry into the Second World War

Once Roosevelt had secured his re-election in November 1940 he began discussing the urgent need for US aid to Britain, which was by this time fighting Nazi Germany alone. The Neutrality Acts did not allow Roosevelt to give aid for which the British could not pay. He managed to get around this by giving Britain 50 First World War destroyers in return for naval bases in British colonies.

Lend-Lease

In March 1941 the **Lend-Lease** Act was passed which allowed aid to be given. This was despite opposition from individuals such as:

- industrialist Henry Ford
- aviator Charles Lindbergh
- leading senators such as Robert La Follette.

Under this scheme the USA supplied war materials to Britain, China and later the Soviet Union. Lend-Lease marked the end of isolationism and US ships escorted British convoys part of the way across the Atlantic as far as Iceland. The mood of the general public shifted further from isolationism when Germany invaded the Soviet Union in June 1941.

The Atlantic Charter

With Lend-Lease underway and news of the German attack on the Soviet Union, Winston Churchill and Franklin Roosevelt met at Placentia Bay in Newfoundland in August. The outcome of the meeting was the **Atlantic Charter**. This amounted to a joint statement of war aims which gave Churchill a pledge that if the USA joined the war, defeating Hitler would be the main priority.

USA + GB allies

The Selective Service Act of September 1940 made it compulsory for all men aged between 21 and 36 to register for military service. This signalled a readiness to prepare for war if and when the time came.

The Atlantic Charter and the Selective Service Act brought the USA a step closer to joining the war.

Japan and Pearl Harbor

It was not support for Britain that brought the USA into the war. It was a surprise attack on the US naval base at Pearl Harbor in Hawaii by Japan on 7 December 1941. Japan attacked the USA for the following reasons:

- The Japanese thought that the USA might help China resist the Japanese invasion of their country. This was made clear when Roosevelt stopped shipments of oil and steel to Japan, without which the Japanese military could not fight for long.
- The Japanese wanted to conquer British and Dutch colonies in the Pacific that could provide oil, rubber and other raw materials to help in the war against China. The only force that could stop them was the American Pacific Fleet which was anchored at Pearl Harbor.

In August 1941 Japan made plans to attack the Americans at Pearl Harbor. Following this attack, Japan's ally, Germany, declared war on the USA on 11 December. The USA was now at war with Japan and Germany.

Mind map

Below are a sample exam-style 12 mark question and the beginnings of a mind map to identify relevant reasons. Read the question and complete the mind map with a sentence of explanation. Then prioritise your reasons by adding numbers to each oval – with 1 as the most important reason and 5 as the least important.

Explain why the USA was not strictly neutral between 1939 and 1941.

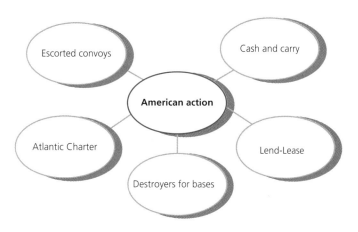

How important?

Below is a sample exam-style 24 mark question which asks you about the importance of a factor. Questions like this can be answered by balancing the way the factor was important against the way in which it was not. A series of statements relevant to the question are given below. Using your own knowledge and the information on the previous pages, decide whether these statements suggest the factor was important or not important and tick the appropriate box.

How important was the Atlantic Charter in bringing the USA into the war in 1941?

	IMPORTANT	NOT IMPORTANT
1. Japan invaded China in 1937.		
2. The cash and carry clause in the Neutrality Act aided Britain and France.		
3. Lend-Lease helped supply war materials to Britain, China and the Soviet Union.		
4. The USA imposed a trade embargo on Japan.		
5. The Atlantic Charter set out war aims between Britain and the USA.		
6. Before 1941, the American public was committed to isolationism.		
7. Japan attacked Pearl Harbor on 7 December 1941.		
8. Germany declared war on the USA on 11 December 1941.		

The impact of the Second World War on American society

Due to continued bombing and invasion, the countries in Europe and the Far East suffered mass civilian casualties. Cities, factories, transportation networks, historic buildings and monuments were destroyed. Many countries were under German or Japanese occupation and subject to their control for up to six years. There was a shortage of goods, particularly food, and many people were used as slave labour. In Europe, millions of people were killed simply because of their religious or political views.

Social changes

The war put an end to the decade-long depression. There was full employment, and very little rationing, ensuring that the majority of US citizens enjoyed increased standards of living. In addition, mainland USA was too far from both Germany and Japan to be bombed. Indeed, almost all the civilian casualties that the USA suffered, estimated to be about 12,000, were caused by accidents in the workplace, particularly in the munitions factories.

War brought new employment opportunities in the factories producing goods for the war, particularly for women and African Americans. By 1944, women formed more than one-third of the workforce, in jobs previously carried out almost exclusively by men. Women were now earning their own money and gained an independence they had never had before.

African Americans were able to advance and move from more manual jobs to take up management posts, which would have been unheard of before the war. There were more African Americans in the armed forces (125,000 served overseas during the Second World War in all branches) and the first black fighter squadron was established, more popularly known as the Tuskegee Airmen.

Impact of the war on minorities

Although there were greater opportunities for African Americans, there was still discrimination in the workplace. Not everyone accepted these social changes. For example, there were several strikes at factories in Detroit by white workers against the employment of African Americans. There was also segregation in the armed forces. Most management positions were still dominated by white males.

Following the attack on Pearl Harbor, Japanese Americans were discriminated against. Rumours persisted that Japanese Americans had assisted the Japanese military in the attack by sending details of the number of ships and troops stationed at Pearl Harbor. Many Japanese Americans living in Hawaii and California were rounded up and sent to internment camps, despite the fact that a number had sons serving in the US armed forces. This was in marked contrast to the treatment of Italian and German Americans.

While some US citizens opposed such treatment, many in the state of California, where the Japanese immigrants had settled, took advantage of the situation and bought up Japanese property cheaply.

The extent of change

Changes for women and African Americans were short-lived. Many women returned to their traditional roles as office workers when the men came home. In addition, despite the advances made by African Americans, segregation remained in the southern states and segregation in the armed forces was not abolished until 1949.

Support for the war

There was a surge in propaganda to get the American public behind the war effort. The fictional character Rosie the Riveter was created to encourage women to fill the vacancies in the factories and shipyards. Hollywood played its part by producing films designed to raise morale, such as *Casablanca* (1942), and documentaries aimed at informing the American public about the war, such as *Why We Fight*, a series of eleven films (1942–1945). High-profile actors joined the armed forces, for example James Stewart was a pilot in the Army Air Force. Radio and popular music was also influential and Roosevelt continued to speak to the American people through his 'fireside chats'.

Make the links

Below are a sample exam-style 12-mark question and a series of relevant reasons that could be used in the answer. Read the question and add a comment and linking phrase to explain each reason and how it relates to the following one.

Explain why the experience of war was different for US citizens between 1941 and 1945.

Reason	Comment and linking phrase leading to the next reason
The war brought full employment and increased the standard of living for many Americans.	
There were no mass civilian casualties caused by the bombing of US cities.	
In contrast to most of Europe and the Far East, the USA was neither invaded nor occupied.	

Turning assertion into argument

Below are a sample exam-style 24-mark question and a series of assertions. Read the question and then add a justification to each of the assertions to turn it into a supported view, so creating an argument.

How far was involvement in the war a positive experience for US citizens?

The American people did not suffer the same hardships that most of the other countries at war suffered ...

_____

_____

The war brought full employment and a higher standard of living to many Americans ...

_____

_____

There was discrimination towards some US citizens ...

_____

_____

The emergence of the USA as a world power by 1945

Revised

The alliance between the USA, Britain and the Soviet Union is often described as a 'marriage of convenience' as it was forged out of necessity. By 1945 the war had transformed the USA and its economy was the strongest in the world. Britain was much weaker than it had been during the inter-war period and was not seen as an equal by the Americans in either economic or military terms.

As the war came to an end ideological differences re-emerged between the West and the Soviet Union. These would develop into the Cold War. The Conference at Yalta in February 1945 and the Potsdam Conference in July/August 1945 determined the development of post-war Europe.

The Yalta Conference, February 1945, in brief

The aim of the Yalta Conference was to discuss what was to happen to Europe after the Second World War. Stalin, Roosevelt and Churchill agreed several things: that Germany and Berlin would be divided into four occupation zones; a war crimes tribunal would be established to put leading Nazis on trial; liberated countries in eastern Europe would be allowed to have free elections.

The Potsdam Conference, July–August 1945, in brief

Many things had changed in six months. The Soviet Union occupied eastern Europe, America successfully tested the atomic bomb and the leaders were Stalin, Truman and Attlee. Germany was demilitarised, Berlin and Germany were divided into four zones as agreed at Yalta and the Nazi Party was banned. The Polish border was moved west, incorporating German territory.

The atomic bomb

Roosevelt died in April 1945 and was replaced by Harry S. Truman, his vice-president. It was Truman who represented the USA at the Potsdam Conference where he received news that a successful test of an atomic bomb had taken place. His decision to use the bomb on Hiroshima and Nagasaki in August 1945 demonstrated its destructive nature and altered the balance of power in Europe in the USA's favour. The power and devastation caused by the two bombs convinced the Japanese leadership to surrender. The objection to the American terms of surrender had been the insistence that Japan lose its emperor. This part of the surrender terms was dropped, making the decision more acceptable to the Japanese government.

The reasons for the use of the atomic bomb have been much debated by historians:

- It was used to reduce the number of US casualties. It was estimated that a US invasion of Japan would have resulted in 1 million US casualties.

- It was to show the world, and the Soviet Union in particular, the destructive power of the new weapon. As the war drew to a close, the Soviet Union and the USA became increasingly suspicious of each other.

- It was to test the effects of the bomb in a real wartime setting. It was an opportunity to see the destructive power of the bomb on cities. This would inform future use of the weapon.

The atomic bomb gave the USA a monopoly on nuclear power, as it took four years for the Soviet Union to produce a nuclear weapon of its own.

The impact of the war on the USA

The USA ended the war in a unique position compared to the other major powers. Its economy had expanded enormously and its industrial capacity was unrivalled. Its technological lead in the war was shown in its production of the world's first atomic weapon. The country was untouched physically by war and had no need for reconstruction. It had more food than it needed, more steel than it could use, full employment, and it possessed the most powerful weapon in the world in the atomic bomb. The USA was now a superpower.

Prioritisation

Below are a sample exam-style 12-mark question and a list of reasons that could be used in the answer. Demonstrating prioritisation is one way of structuring the answer to an 'Explain why' question. Using your own knowledge and the information contained on the previous page, decide the order of priority you would give to these factors. Write numbers in the spectrum below to indicate their importance and, beneath each, briefly justify that factor's placement, demonstrating why you feel some factors are more important than others.

Explain why the war strengthened the USA's position as a world power.

1. Relative weakness of other countries, particularly Britain

2. Economic and industrial growth

3. The USA was untouched by the war

4. Development of the atomic bomb demonstrated the USA's technological lead

5. Use of the atomic bomb demonstrated its power and showed the rest of the world that the USA should be feared

Most important   Least important

 Make the links   **(a)**

Below are a sample exam-style 12-mark question and a series of relevant reasons that could be used in the answer. Read the question and add a comment and linking phrase to explain each reason and how it relates to the following one.

Explain why the USA used the atomic bomb on Japan in August 1945.

Reason	Comment and linking phrase leading to the next reason
To bring a quick end to the war.	
To show the Soviet Union and the rest of the world its destructive power.	
To test the bomb in a wartime setting.	

Exam focus

Below is a sample A-grade essay for a 24-mark question. Read it and the examiner's comments around it.

How far was society changed by the USA's involvement in the war between 1941 and 1945?

Good concise opening paragraph that demonstrates an understanding of social change but also its limitations.

The war certainly had a profound impact on American society, particularly on traditional gender roles and the opportunities available to minorities such as African Americans. However, these changes were not universal and were dependent on issues such as location within the USA and level of discrimination.

These two sentences highlight the changing role of women in the workforce with a direct comparison with their role before the outbreak of the war.

As the war took many men from the factory floor, their positions needed to be filled in order to maintain war production. Many of these jobs were taken by women and increasing numbers of African Americans. Jobs that were usually considered male-dominated work were now being undertaken by women. This marked a significant change and by 1944 women formed more than one-third of the workforce. Now women were earning real money in their own right and it gave them a sense of independence that they had never experienced before.

This shows the impact the war had on African Americans in the workplace and in the armed forces.

African Americans had greater opportunities to climb the social ladder as they were able to move into management positions alongside white Americans. There were opportunities too in the armed forces and a greater role for African Americans, particularly in the Army Air Force where the 'Tuskegee Airmen' became the first black pilots of the war. Both women and African Americans obtained skilled employment in the factories producing goods for war.

Here it points out the skills that were obtained as a result of the war.

This balances advances made by women and African Americans by showing the limitations of their social progress, particularly in industry.

However, despite the fact that women and African Americans improved their employment opportunities, senior positions were still dominated by white males, particularly in management jobs and in the armed forces. Race and gender discrimination was evident in some industries, particularly the car workers in Detroit, who went out on strike over the issue of jobs being given to African Americans.

This details the problems that Japanese Americans had in contrast to the advances made by women and African Americans because of the war.

Discrimination increased towards Asian Americans, particularly Japanese Americans, after the attack on Pearl Harbor. Rumours became widespread that Japanese Americans had assisted the attack on Pearl Harbor and they were rounded up and placed in internment camps for the duration of the war, despite the fact that many had sons already serving in the American armed forces. In addition, little changed in the southern states as segregation remained in place long after the war ended.

Once the war was over, both women and African Americans reverted to their traditional roles. The women returned to office and secretarial work and African Americans went back to non-management positions. The armed forces remained segregated throughout the war despite the fact that they had fought against the Nazis to rid Europe of a racist tyrant.

This shows that the social advances were short lived and only really covered the duration of the war.

The fact that the war changed American society is not in question. However, the level of change was largely dependent on where people lived in the United States. For example, there were opportunities for social advancement in the North through increasing job opportunities but very little changed attitudes in the southern states as segregation remained the norm. Women gained a greater sense of independence and financial freedom that they had not experienced before but this was short-lived as many returned to their traditional domestic roles when the war ended and the men returned home. Japanese Americans fared badly between 1941 and 1945 as they were regarded as a danger and locked away in internment camps.

A strong conclusion that draws together the main points but also suggests that the war had a greater impact on social change in the decades that followed.

24/24

A good solid answer to the question which shows the candidate has a good understanding of the impact the war had on American society. The answer contains supporting evidence and the detail required and provides balance. The links back to the question on social change are evident throughout and the conclusion ties everything together. It would therefore receive full marks.

Reverse engineering

The best essays are based on careful plans. Read this essay and the examiner's comments and try to work out the general points of the plan used to write this essay. Once you have done this, note down the specific examples used to support each point.

Glossary

Alphabet Agencies Organisations set up under Roosevelt's New Deal programme to help combat the Great Depression.

America First Committee An organisation established in 1940 which campaigned against future American involvement in the war in Europe and promoted isolationism and neutrality.

American Protective Association (APA) An organisation set up in 1887 to oppose Catholic influence in the USA.

Anti-Semitic Discriminating against Jewish people.

Anti-trust suits Legal action taken against monopolistic businesses.

Asiatic Barred Zone An area including much of Asia and the Pacific islands, identified by the 1917 Immigration Act, from which inhabitants were not allowed to emigrate to the USA.

Atlantic Charter Policy statement by Britain and the United States in August 1941 that set out Allied goals for the post-war world.

Barker-Karpis gang Depression-era gang which was involved in bank robberies and kidnapping between 1931 and 1935.

Bicameral Means 'two chambers', and can be used to refer to Congress which is made up of two houses.

Bolshevik Revolution The Marxist–Leninist inspired uprising which brought the Communists to power in Russia in 1917.

Bonus Army/Bonus Marchers First World War veterans had been issued bonus certificates by Congress in 1924 for $1000 to be paid in 1945. Because of the depression, many of these veterans wanted Congress to agree to pay the bonus earlier and they marched to Washington, D.C. and set up camp in protest.

Bootlegging Includes the manufacturing, transporting and selling of illegal alcohol.

Boss system Based around a very powerful individual who exerts political power in a particular area, but may or may not be a formally elected politician, e.g. Tammany Hall in New York.

Buying on margin Refers to the purchase of stocks whereby the buyer puts down a small percentage with the broker providing the additional cost in the form of a loan.

Capitalist economic system An economic and political system in which a country's trade and industry are controlled by private owners for profit, rather than by the state.

Central Powers The collective term for Germany, Austria–Hungary, the Ottoman Empire (and later Bulgaria) during the First World War.

Checks and balances The term given to devices within the US Constitution designed to ensure that no one branch/part of government or individual can exert too much power.

Court packing scheme Franklin Roosevelt's response to the Supreme Court decisions over some of his New Deal policies. This called for an increase in Supreme Court justices from nine to fifteen and the compulsory retirement of justices at the age of 70. This would allow Roosevelt to 'pack' the court with six new justices who he believed would help his policies go unchallenged. This was defeated by Congress in 1937.

Defrocked A term used for priests who are officially removed from their job. They are no longer able to carry out their religious duties.

Dollar diplomacy An approach to foreign policy by the US government which emphasised the use of money and business in order to exert influence, rather than through military power.

Dust Bowl The name given to the region of the Midwest that included Colorado, Kansas, Oklahoma and Texas which was worst hit by drought, soil erosion and high winds that caused huge dust storms.

Eugenicists People who support ways of 'improving' the population. However, this may include ideas linked to racial segregation and preventing people with hereditary illnesses from reproducing.

Fixed term elections The idea that a particular type of election will always be held at the same regular interval, e.g. the US Presidential election is always held every four years in November.

Free coinage The free coinage of silver was campaigned for by the Populists in the hope that it would inflate the economy and in particular help the farmers.

Gold Standard The idea that the currency should be linked to a fixed quantity of gold.

Impeach To vote (in the House of Representatives) to put the President on trial (by the Senate). In the period 1890–1945 no US president was impeached, but it remained one of the potential 'checks and balances' of the Constitution.

Isolationism An approach to foreign policy which in essence meant the USA stayed out of the affairs of other countries.

Laissez-faire An approach to economics associated with the free market and very limited government intervention in the economy.

Lend-Lease An agreement that would allow Britain to receive American loans and material aid to help fight against Nazism.

Liberty League An American political organisation formed in 1934, primarily by conservative Democrats, to oppose the New Deal policies of Franklin D. Roosevelt.

Margin call A demand by the broker that the lender deposit more money or pay off the loan to cover the debt.

Monopolies Areas of the economy dominated by one company or business leader.

Nationalisation The process of a government taking control of a company or industry.

Nativist A confusing term in that American Indians have been referred to as 'Native Americans', but in this book the term refers broadly to white Americans whose ancestors had emigrated to the USA in the first half of the nineteenth century or earlier. Such people tended to have northern and western European origins, and wished to distinguish themselves from the groups who came to the USA in the second half of the nineteenth century and later, from southern/eastern European or Asian backgrounds.

Naturalised Someone who has become a citizen of the country to which they have moved.

New immigrants Essentially people coming from southern and eastern Europe and Asia in the latter decades of the nineteenth century and early twentieth century.

Noble experiment The term often used to describe Prohibition.

Normalcy Often thought to be a word that did not exist until Warren Harding used it to outline what his main policy as President would be in the 1920 campaign. He meant that he wanted to take back the USA to the way things had been before the war, i.e. not intervening too much in foreign affairs and focusing on domestic issues.

Open Door policy Usually refers to the 1899 policy of Secretary of State John Hay who wished to maintain US trade with China and wanted other imperial powers to recognise this.

Padrone system This originated among Italian immigrants and is very similar to the 'boss' system.

Padrones acted as middlemen between employers and immigrants who needed jobs, but were often unscrupulous and exploited immigrants to their own ends.

Poverty line Minimum amount of income required to subsist in a particular country.

Rugged individualism A phrase used by Herbert Hoover who believed that all individuals could succeed on their own and that government did not need to intervene in the economic lives of the American people.

Sharecroppers Tenant farmers who paid their landlords a share of the crop they produced.

Speakeasies Establishments that illegally sold alcohol.

Tariffs A tax imposed on imported goods and services.

Temperance groups Organisations that campaigned for a partial or complete reduction in the use of alcohol.

Triangle Shirtwaist Fire Factory disaster in New York City in 1911 in which 146 people died (mainly female garment workers).

Veto In this case refers to the right of the US President to unilaterally stop Congress from passing a law, although that veto can be overridden should Congress muster a two-thirds majority in response.

Volstead Act The legislation passed by Congress which covered the precise detail of how Prohibition would be enforced.

Voluntarism The policy of the Hoover administration that advocated charitable help from businesses, churches and local communities rather than relying on government intervention to help relieve those hit by the depression.

WASP A term meaning White Anglo-Saxon Protestant.

Wet A term used to define someone who was against the prohibition of alcohol, or a state that had not banned alcohol.

World Revolution The Marxist idea that capitalism should be overthrown in every country of the world. This idea made Americans much more wary about the intentions of socialists and communists in their own country.

Yellow dog contracts Written agreements between workers and employers by which the worker agrees not to be a member of a union.

Yellow Press Derogatory term for the popular press in the USA during the period – broadly equivalent to the term 'tabloid press' – referring to papers which carried eye-catching headlines and stories based on limited research.

Timeline

1890   Sherman Anti-Trust Act.

Sherman Silver Purchase Act.

McKinley Tariff.

Jacob Riis's *How the other half lives* published.

Closing of the frontier.

1896   William McKinley (Republican) elected President.

1898   Spanish-American War.

1901   McKinley assassinated – Theodore Roosevelt becomes President.

1902   Newlands Act.

Platt Amendment establishes US protection of Cuba.

1903   Federal court dissolves Northern Securities Company.

1904   Theodore Roosevelt (Republican) elected President.

Roosevelt Corollary.

1911   Triangle Shirtwaist Fire.

1912   Woodrow Wilson (Democrat) elected President.

1913   Sixteenth Amendment (income tax).

Seventeenth Amendment (direct election of senators).

General Huerta seizes power in Mexico.

1914   Ludlow Massacre.

Clayton Anti-Trust Act.

Panama Canal completed.

Start of First World War.

1917   Zimmermann Telegram.

USA declares war on Germany.

1918   Wilson announces Fourteen Points peace plan.

End of First World War.

1919   Paris Peace Conference.

Versailles Treaty signed.

League of Nations set up.

Eighteenth Amendment ratified (Prohibition).

Boston Police strike.

Chicago Race Riot.

Volstead Act.

1920   Nineteenth Amendment ratified (female suffrage).

US Senate rejects Versailles Treaty.

Palmer Raids and Red Scare.

Sacco and Vanzetti tried.

Harding (Republican) elected President.

1923   Calvin Coolidge becomes President after Harding dies in office.

1924   Coolidge (Republican) elected President.

Dawes Plan.

Immigration Restriction Act.

1928   Herbert Hoover (Republican) elected President.

Kellogg–Briand Pact.

1929   Wall Street Crash.

Young Plan.

1930   Dust storms signal the beginning of drought conditions in the Midwest.

1931   The Great Depression begins as banks fail and unemployment rises.

Al Capone is arrested and tried for tax evasion.

1932   Unemployment reaches 25 per cent as the depression bites hard.

Hoover is defeated in the presidential election by Franklin D. Roosevelt.

1933   Roosevelt launches the First New Deal.

Hitler is made Chancellor of Germany.

Prohibition is repealed by the Twenty-first Amendment.

1935   The Second New Deal begins.

1936   Roosevelt re-elected.

1939   Germany invades Poland, sparking a general European war.

The Neutrality Act is amended to allow arms trade on a cash and carry basis.

1941   Lend-Lease is introduced to help Britain fight Nazi Germany.

The Atlantic Charter is signed by Churchill and Roosevelt.

Germany attacks the Soviet Union.

Japan attacks Pearl Harbor in Hawaii.

Germany declares war on the USA.

1944   US war production reaches its peak, supplying war materials for both Britain and the Soviet Union.

D-Day landings begin the liberation of western Europe.

Roosevelt elected for a fourth term.

1945   Roosevelt, Churchill and Stalin meet at Yalta to discuss plans for the post-war world.

Roosevelt dies in April and is succeeded by Harry S. Truman.

Germany surrenders in May but war against Japan continues.

War against Japan is brought to an end when two atomic bombs are dropped on Hiroshima and Nagasaki. The USA is now the world's first nuclear power.

Answers

Section 1: The USA, 1890–c1920

Page 5, Turning assertion into argument: suggested answer
... because the US President is Commander-in-Chief of the armed forces.

... because they could initiate legislative programmes to be put through Congress.

... and could appoint Supreme Court judges as well as members of the Cabinet.

Page 7, Turning statements into reasons: suggested answer

STATEMENT	REASON
McKinley's campaign was well funded and well organised	... which allowed him to pay for posters to help his campaign.
The Republicans supported the gold standard and *laissez-faire* economic policies	... which won him support from big business, wealthy farmers and urban workers.
The Democrats supported the free coinage of silver and lower tariffs	... which appealed to rural farmers rather than big business owners, who in turn backed the Republicans.
McKinley's foreign policy seemed likely to help the Cubans	... which appealed to the public who felt that the Cubans had been treated badly by the Spanish.
McKinley won New York State	... which was crucial because it had the highest number of electoral college votes in the Union.
The Democrats were in power when the panic and downturn of 1893 happened	... which meant that many voters blamed them for the economic downturn.

Page 9, Economic, political or social factors?
Economic: 1,4. Political: 6,7. Social: 2,3,5.

Page 9, Identify an argument

Paragraph 1 is a typical lower-level answer which is descriptive, makes factual statements which are not used as evidence to support argument, and includes assertion which is not supported by evidence. Paragraph 2 is a much stronger answer. It starts by addressing the question directly, puts forward relevant argument and backs up argument with detailed evidence.

Page 11, Make the links: suggested answer

Reason	Comment and linking phrase leading to the next reason
Raw materials and infrastructure	Plentiful raw materials such as coal and iron ore which could be found in Pennsylvania, for example, provided essential ingredients for the mass production of steel, which was dominated in the late eighteenth and early nineteenth centuries by Andrew Carnegie.
Entrepreneurs and innovators	Entrepreneurs and innovators such as Carnegie, who utilised the Bessemer process in order to produce steel more efficiently, contributed greatly to the USA becoming a major industrial power, and these manufacturers were helped by the sympathetic attitudes of the federal government.
Attitudes of federal government	Federal government during the period was dominated by the Republican Party which favoured *laissez-faire* policies, which in turn allowed big business to expand.

Page 11, Complete the paragraph: suggested answer

Andrew Carnegie dominated the steel industry and adopted the Bessemer process which made the large-scale production of steel much easier. Similarly, J.P. Morgan became so powerful in banking and finance that he played a major part in cutting deals which prevented economic disaster in 1907.

Page 13, Complete the paragraph: suggested answer

Roosevelt's administration only brought 44 anti-trust suits against companies, and Taft's administration only brought 90 anti-trust suits against big business, although one involved US Steel, the largest corporation in the USA.

Page 13, Develop the detail: suggested answer

It can be argued in terms of their attitudes towards the power of big business that Theodore Roosevelt was not as Progressive as Taft or Wilson. Roosevelt intervened on the side of the workers in the miners' strike of 1902 **which resulted in a 10 per cent pay increase and nine-hour day for the miners**. He also brought a lot of land under government protection to stop it being exploited by big business **by using the 1891 Forest Reserve Act to protect 150 million acres of forest**, and used **the 1890 Sherman Act** to dissolve a railroad company, **Northern Securities,** and other trusts. A lot more trusts – **90** – however, were prosecuted when Taft was president including the biggest corporation in the country, **US Steel**, and Taft also brought more land under his protection **using the 1910 General Withdrawal Act**. Wilson actually improved on the laws which investigated the trusts **with the 1914 Clayton Anti-trust Act** and introduced a shorter, **eight-hour** working day for railroad workers **with the 1916 Adamson Act**. It could be argued that he achieved more in this area than Roosevelt too.

Page 15, Turning assertion into argument: suggested answer

... he came up with the Roosevelt Corollary which justified US intervention in the Americas.

... to some extent he moved towards the 'dollar diplomacy' approach.

... he committed the USA to war with Spain over Cuba, which resulted in huge economic gains for the country.

Page 17, You're the examiner

Level 5: Directly addresses the question and gives a clear line of argument, while putting forward detailed evidence such as the Zimmermann Telegram to support this argument. The last sentence, however, hints that German aggression may have been a convenient cover for the US entry into the war, and implies that the essay will consider other factors, thus providing balance.

Page 19, Long-term or short-term?

Long-term: 1,2,3. Short-term: 4,5,6.

Page 19, Turning assertion into argument: suggested answer

... for example Myron T. Herrick, who lost his position as governor of Ohio because of such pressure.

Many breweries in the USA were owned by German Americans, and Americans did not want to seem to be supporting industries that might donate money to the German government.

Henry Ford, for example, backed Prohibition in the hope that it would improve worker absence and result in his workers having more money to spend on Ford cars.

Section 2: The USA, c1920–1929

Page 23, Make the links: suggested answer

Reason	Comment and linking phrase leading to the next reason
Fears of anarchism and communism had become greater since the assassination of President McKinley and the Russian Revolution of 1917.	Such fears seemed to be justified when bombs were sent to prominent figures in 1919 …
A number of mail bombs were sent in April/May 1919, including one which exploded at the house of Attorney General Palmer.	Palmer was not injured by the bomb, but he decided to launch a number of raids in the winter of 1918/1919 to clamp down on left-wing agitation …
Palmer harboured ambitions of running for president and it could be argued that thousands of arrests and deportations would go down well with the public.	Palmer's predictions of further violence in May 1920 came to nothing and this helped to scupper his political ambitions.

Page 23, Specific or underlying?

Underlying: 1,5. Specific: 2,3,4,6.

Page 25, Long-term or short-term?

Long-term: 1,3. Short-term: 2,4,5,6.

Page 25, Identify an argument

Paragraph 1 is a typical lower-level answer which is descriptive, makes factual statements which are not used as evidence to support argument, and includes assertion which is not supported by evidence. Paragraph 2 is a much stronger answer. It starts by addressing the question directly, puts forward relevant argument and backs up argument with detailed evidence. It also includes other factors to be examined which suggests the answer will have balance, and links the pre-war period with the war itself and the Bolshevik Revolution.

Page 27, Make the links: suggested answer

Reason	Comment and linking phrase leading to the next reason
Assembly line production:	Henry Ford had originally set up assembly line production in Detroit in 1913 which he utilised to manufacture cars on a massive scale.
Manufacture of cars:	The manufacture of cars had a huge knock-on effect on other parts of the economy, creating a huge demand for materials such as leather and glass. It also led to a vast expansion of road building to which federal governments contributed.
Federal road building:	The Federal Aid Highway Act of 1921 helped to set up a national highway system of roads, with more than $75 million being spent within a year which helped to sustain car production.

Page 27, Eliminate irrelevance

Eliminate the sentence: Henry Ford set up the first moving assembly line in 1913 in Detroit and became famous for building the Model T car. By 1929 one cost as little as $290.

Page 29, Develop the detail: suggested answer

It can be argued that the USA before 1890 had been made up essentially of people who had come from northern and western Europe**an countries such as Britain**, but that after 1890 a greater proportion of immigrants were coming from southern and eastern European countries **such as Italy** and from parts of Asia. These immigrants generally held religious beliefs which were not Protestant, **for example Catholicism and Judaism**, and political values that may have been different from those subscribed to by most Americans. The impact of the Emergency Quota Act of 1921 and the Johnson–Reed Act of 1924, **which fixed quotas at 2 per cent of those groups living in the USA in 1890**, was to massively reduce the total number of all immigrants entering the country, but to disproportionately cut the numbers entering from southern and eastern Europe and Asia.

Page 31, Identify an argument

Paragraph 1 is a stronger answer. It starts by addressing the question directly, puts forward relevant argument and backs up argument with detailed evidence. Paragraph 2 is a typical lower-level answer which is descriptive, makes factual statements which are not used as evidence to support argument, and includes assertion which is not supported by evidence.

Page 33, Turning statements into reasons: suggested answer

STATEMENT	REASON
The poorest 40% of families received 12.5% of the country's income during the 1920s ...	... which meant that many were unable to afford consumer goods.
Farm prices fell once the war had ended ...	... which meant that many rural areas suffered from poverty during the 1920s and were unable to take advantage of the production of cheaper consumer goods.
The Fordney–McCumber tariff of 1922 raised prices on foreign food coming into the USA ...	... which led to other countries imposing tariffs on American agricultural products which made it more difficult for farmers to export.
Prohibition was introduced in the 1920s ...	... which resulted in a drop in the demand for grain.
Agriculture became more mechanised ...	... which led to unemployment in rural areas.
Unions were weak during the period ...	... which meant that low-paid workers were unable to improve their situation.
Lots of banks failed during the 1920s ...	... which meant that many investors lost their savings.
Many African Americans worked as sharecroppers in the South ...	... which ensured they remained as debtors unable to escape the cycle of poverty.

Page 33, Complete the paragraph: suggested answer

...**the Fordney–McCumber tariff on American agricultural products which made it more difficult for farmers to export, and Prohibition damaged grain production as the demand from the distillers and brewers simply stopped. In 1924 alone about 600,000 farmers lost their farms, and by 1929 the agricultural workforce had fallen by 5 per cent.**

Page 35, Develop the detail: suggested answer

One reason why the USA became less interventionist was because **117,000 Americans were** killed during the First World War. The peace-making efforts of Woodrow Wilson had also not gone down well with the American people **with major opposition to US involvement in the League of Nations and to the terms of the Treaty of Versailles. Hearst newspapers also opposed continued intervention in European affairs.**

Page 35, You're the examiner

Level 5: Directly addresses the question and gives a clear line of argument, while putting forward detailed evidence such as the Monroe Doctrine and the occupation of Haiti to support this argument, as well as exhibiting balance regarding Europe. The strongly put argument and judgement that US policy was not entirely isolationist also implies a confidence which is typical of a Level 5 answer.

Section 3: The Great Depression and the New Deal, 1929–1941

Page 39, Identify an argument

Paragraph 2 contains the argument; paragraph 1 is descriptive.

Page 41, Long-term or short-term

Long-term: 1,4,5. Short-term: 2,3,6.

Page 41, Turning assertion into argument: suggested answer

Mechanisation increased unemployment in these sectors and wages were kept low as employers tried to maximise profits.

This discouraged saving as a buy-now-pay-later mentality developed. When the stock market crashed and workers were laid off it became difficult for these people to meet their debts and many of the goods were repossessed.

By the end of 1928 those people who could afford the larger consumer items such as cars, fridges and washing machines already had them. The drop in demand created a large surplus of goods that nobody wanted and so production was scaled down, leading to unemployment.

Page 43, Turning assertion into argument: suggested answer

… due to overproduction following the First World War. Prohibition added to their problems as they could no longer sell grain to brewers and distillers. The tariffs set by government also hit farmers hard as they could not export grain to foreign countries that had put up their own tariffs in response.

A series of droughts caused crops to fail and the Dust Bowl that followed blew away all the top soil.

… as 25 per cent of the working population became unemployed by 1933. Many lost their homes and roamed America looking for employment, thereby separating them from their families.

Page 45, Develop the detail: suggested answer

Hoover's treatment of the Bonus Marchers in the summer of 1932, so close to the election, undoubtedly had an impact on his electoral chances, but this was more the final straw than the main cause of public discontent. His staunch belief in rugged individualism, coupled with his view that supporting businesses through the Reconstruction and Finance Corporation would in turn revive the economy, was seen as a huge failure. **By the end of 1932, 25 per cent of the working-age population was unemployed. This is further demonstrated by his support of voluntarism as he believed that direct aid would lead to greater dependency on the government.** His decision to support higher tariffs caused further damage to the failing economy too **as this caused other countries to put up protective tariffs in response, thereby hampering American exports.**

Page 47, Turning statements into reasons: suggested answers

STATEMENT	REASON
The Public Works Administration (PWA) was created in 1933.	It was a large-scale public works programme to create employment on building projects such as roads, bridges and housing.
The Works Progress Administration (WPA) had widespread appeal.	It employed millions of unskilled men in building roads, public buildings and parks and also helped employ writers, musicians and artists in drama and literary projects.
The Tennessee Valley Authority (TVA) was successful.	It spanned seven states, built several dams to provide cheap hydro-electric power, prevented flooding and provided irrigation to farmlands, and created employment.
The Civilian Conservation Corps (CCC) helped young men.	It provided employment for young unmarried men aged 18–25 in conservation work, such as creating parks and planting trees. More than 2 million young men were employed between 1933 and 1941.

Page 47, You're the examiner

The paragraph quickly links to the question by reflecting it in the first sentence. There is some detail of various Alphabet Agencies and their impact on reducing unemployment. There is some balance as it goes on to discuss how this was limited but does not go into as much detail, e.g. CCC pay was low but it does not state what the pay was ($30 per month). It would therefore be placed at the top of Level 3.

Page 49, How important?

Important: 1,4,5. Not important: 2,3.

Page 49, Identify an argument

Paragraph 2 contains the argument; paragraph 1 is descriptive.

Page 51, Creating a Venn diagram

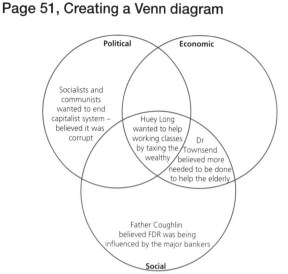

Page 51, Make the links: suggested answer

Reason	Comment and linking phrase leading to the next reason
Dr Francis Townsend was concerned with the impact the depression was having on the elderly and felt the New Deal was not doing enough to address this.	He put forward a plan that would give everyone over 60 $200 each month on the condition that they spent it within 30 days. This, he believed, would also stimulate the economy.
Father Charles Coughlin felt that Roosevelt was being influenced by the bankers in producing his New Deal policies.	He called for a nationalisation of industry, greater use of silver coinage and inflationary measures.
Huey Long was a major critic of the New Deal and felt it did not go far enough in helping the working class.	He launched the 'Share Our Wealth' campaign in 1934 which promoted a $5000 homestead allowance and a minimum wage of $2500 per year to all workers. This would be paid by increase in taxation on the most wealthy in the USA.

Page 53, Make the links: suggested answer

Reason	Comment and linking phrase leading to the next reason
The Republican Party was opposed to New Deal policies.	They opposed many of Roosevelt's policies during the 1930s, believing government intervention had gone too far, was un-American and socialist in nature. They were supported by some big business leaders in this belief.
Big business resented government intervention.	The right to collective bargaining angered business leaders and they resented government interference in trade. They challenged Roosevelt's policies through the courts, often with success, which caused him to refine his policies.
Some states feared that the New Deal threatened their rights under the Constitution.	Opposition from state legislatures came particularly from southern states. When the New Deal provided some public assistance to black southerners and when Roosevelt's wife, Eleanor, spoke out against racial discrimination, white southerners believed the New Deal was a threat to states' rights and their supremacy in the South.
The Liberty League wanted to curb growing presidential power.	The main aim of the League was to uphold the Constitution against New Deal policies that might undermine it and give too much power to the president. Its aim was to challenge FDR in the 1936 presidential election and when it failed, by a large margin, it began to collapse.

Page 53, Complete the paragraph: suggested answer

Certainly the striking down of the Agricultural Adjustment Act (AAA) and the National Industrial Recovery Act (NIRA) caused Roosevelt to rethink his policies and draft legislation much more carefully during the Second New Deal. Roosevelt sought a dramatic way around Supreme Court opposition through his court packing scheme, which damaged his relationship with Congress.

Page 55, Turning assertion into argument: suggested answer

… because many of the reasons put forward for the ban on alcohol, such as increased productivity, better health and a reduction in crime had not materialised.

… when a series of newspaper articles appeared in the *Washington Post* entitled 'The Man in the Green Hat'. The man, George Cassiday, had been supplying senators and congressmen, the very people making Prohibition laws, with illegal alcohol for ten years.

... because it had cost the federal government $11 billion in lost taxation. In addition, it cost more than $300 million to enforce through the federal prohibition agencies and the coastguard.

Page 57, Make the links: suggested answer

Reason	Comment and linking phrase leading to the next reason
Funding for law enforcement was poor.	The amount of money available to the federal government for law enforcement, amid the grip of the Great Depression, was a fraction compared to that of organised crime.
Bribery and corruption at the federal level was still a major problem.	This was especially the case during the depression and this meant that crime gangs were protected.
Most crimes were the responsibility of individual states.	Murder, robbery and a host of other crimes came under state law and corruption at this level meant that the federal government had no control in these areas. This was shown in the trial of Al Capone who was never convicted of murder as he had corrupted most state officials.

Page 57, Complete the paragraph: suggested answer

Many crimes came under state law so the federal government had no control in these areas. Dillinger and Kelly were part of Prohibition-era gangs that operated in the Midwest and not part of organised crime targeted by the government. Bribery and corruption at the federal level meant that crime gangs were protected which made enforcement difficult. The amount of money that organised crime could generate was much more than the federal government could provide for law enforcement during the depression era.

Section 4: The impact of the Second World War on the USA, 1941–1945

Page 61, You're the examiner

This paragraph is quite detailed in its explanation. It draws a direct comparison to the issues that brought the USA into the First World War, such as arms sales and citizens travelling on ships of warring nations. It also attempts to balance the answer by including the re-introduction of the cash and carry clause to show that the Neutrality Acts did not necessarily mean America was neutral. However, it is not as detailed on this point and so would receive Level 4.

Page 63, How important?

Important: 3,4,5,7. Not important: 1,2,6,8.

Page 65, Make the links: suggested answer

Reason	Comment and linking phrase leading to the next reason
The war brought full employment and increased the standard of living for many Americans.	War brought new employment opportunities in the factories producing goods for the war, particularly for women and African Americans.
There were no mass civilian casualties caused by the bombing of US cities.	The USA was too far from both Germany and Japan to be bombed. Almost all the civilian casualties that the USA suffered, estimated to be about 12,000, were caused by accidents in the workplace, particularly in munitions factories.
In contrast to most of Europe and the Far East, the USA was neither invaded nor occupied.	They did not suffer food shortages and were not used as slave labour or killed for their religious beliefs.

Page 65, Turning assertion into argument

... for a number of reasons. Mainland USA was too far from both Japan and Germany and so Americans did not have to contend with bombing raids on their cities. In addition, the USA was not occupied by Japanese or German forces.

... due to increased war production and the fact that there was very little rationing of food and other consumer goods.

... for example, there were several strikes in Detroit by white workers against the employment of African Americans and, following the attack on Pearl Harbor, Japanese Americans were rounded up and sent to internment camps.

Page 67, Make the links: suggested answer

Reason	Comment and linking phrase leading to the next reason
To bring a quick end to the war.	It was estimated that a US invasion of Japan would have resulted in 1 million US casualties.
To show the Soviet Union and the rest of the world its destructive power.	As the war drew to a close, both the Soviet Union and the USA became increasingly suspicious of each other.
To test the bomb in a wartime setting.	It was an opportunity to see the destructive power of the bomb on cities. This would inform future use of the weapon.